SULLIVAN, RICHARD

The story of Ramses
87-133 $14.95

DATE DUE			
Fac			

The Queen Nefertari

Ramses II enjoyed the company of innumerable women. But he revered only one, Nefertari. She was his first wife and, for as long as she lived, the Queen of Egypt. There are two accounts of her lineage. In one she is thought to have been a daughter of the provincial nobility and part of a small harem given to the boy Ramses by his father, Seti I. The second, more likely account, identifies Nefertari as Ramses' own sister, the daughter of Queen Tuaa.

Nefertari's portraits show us a woman of graceful bearing and the tall, supple elegance of her race. It is not surprising that Ramses II, considered the most handsome of Egypt's kings, chose as his queen, Nefertari, whose name means 'the most beautiful.'

The Story of

RAMSES

RICHARD SULLIVAN

THE EDWIN MELLEN PRESS
LEWISTON/QUEENSTON

The Story of Ramses
by Richard Sullivan

Designed and illustrated by Beth Kroecker

ISBN 0-88946-046-9

Box 450
Lewiston, New York
14092   USA

Box 67
Queenston, Ontario
L0S 1L0   CANADA

Printed in The United States of America

MAPS

TABLE OF CONTENTS

For help in preparing this book, it is a pleasure to thank Richard Boyer, Philip Amos, Herbert Richardson, Peter Beyer, Beth Kroecker, and Dawn M. Reitz. Also, please acknowledge Betty Brown, Terri Wegerski, Shirley House, and Claire Lega. The maps have been drawn to varying scales by Josette Salles, who still does not need glasses.

Dr. Richard D. Sullivan
Professor of Classics (Ret.)
University of Saskatchewan
Professor of History (Adjunct)
Simon Fraser University

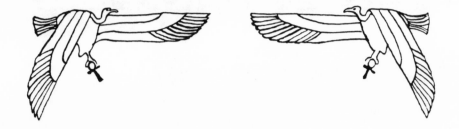

Chapter 1

The Setting

LIFE IN ANCIENT EGYPT

Guests at a banquet in Ancient Egypt often were given a lotus blossom. A pot of scented ointment was placed on the head.

The Geography of Egypt

Of all the sayings about Egypt, probably the most vivid and true is one attributed to the Greek geographer Hecataeus some twenty-five centuries ago: "Egypt is the gift of the Nile" (Herodotus 2.5).

Egypt proper is the Nile Valley, from the first cataract north to Memphis, near the modern Cairo; that's less than 400 miles. The second portion is the Delta, from Memphis north to the Mediterranean Sea, some 100 miles. The third element is the surrounding desert.

The total area amounts to 400,000 square miles, but only 8500 square miles of that lie in the fertile Delta, and only 4800 compose the Nile Valley proper.

The rest is desert, then and now: the Arabian Desert, the Western Desert, and the Libyan Sahara. Here lies a cushion from invaders, but also a permanent heartache. The population stares wide-eyed out into the sands, murmuring that water could convert the permanent sunlight to crops.

Nobody invades Egypt lightly, as Rommel knew and as Ramses did before him. However, once you get inside, that lovely water beckons, and the Romans said *qui Nilum bibit bibet:* "Whoever drinks of the Nile will do so again."

The Nile ranks as the longest river in the world, even the part that shows. As the ancients said, its head hides itself from the sun. It flows 4,000 miles, from the Kagera River in Tanganyika, then from Lake Victoria, up to the Mediterranean. The Blue Nile, the White Nile, and other pretty names all describe the same muddy stream. The ancients probably knew where the headwaters were.

Of that 4,000 miles, only 400 traverse Egypt proper, from 24 to 31 degrees north latitude, from the first of its six cataracts to the

Mediterranean Sea. But that is the most important portion of the highlands of Ethiopia spreads out over the sands of the Nile Valley and the Delta to form one of the most fertile soils on earth. That steady deposit especially benefits the Delta, which Herodotus in the fifth century before Christ called "the land which is always rising." That's not from deposit of debris, as with us, but from thick, rich mud, the staff of life.

Egyptians have used that mud since deepest prehistory and they still do; they can even build cool, sturdy, rainproof housing from it.

Entire cities lie buried in that mud, or rise partly out of it. We excavated portions of two in the Naukratis Project, about three years ago, and my own greatest surprise lay in the quantity of materials from the reign of Ramses II. Every village has its fragment of an obelisk or decree of his, and the fields still regularly yield the little figurines called shawabtis. Everywhere one can see the ruins of cities known by name and with their own histories. About this time every year they become especially dramatic as the flood covers the rest of the Delta. Rising out of the water are the city-mounds, some villages or roads, and just the eyebrows of the donkeys.

In Egypt, you don't have to "think sun" as we do; it's there. Outside of the Delta, the sun shines 365 days a year. The climate is one of the most stable in the world because of the latitude, of course, not far above the equator, but also because of the longitude. Egypt lies too far west and north to be much affected by the monsoons from the Indian Ocean. It's also too far south for the worst of the Mediterranean storms. They can hit the Delta, but they break up before penetrating the Nile Valley.

The result? You can count on the weather. When Ramses scheduled one of his six Jubilees--a kind of giant picnic to celebrate continuance

of the reign--he could order what he fancied, and nobody worried about awnings. We have vivid records of the resulting festivals.

Egyptian Society

It's hard to overestimate the effect of the geography and climate on Egypt. If one relies on a river, he or she takes what it gives. Here, it gives a Nile Valley as little as ten miles wide. The Valley proper is never more than 31 miles wide.

That means Egyptians had quite an intimate society, and people had better get along together. Society will enforce its norms intensely. Anyone familiar with village life in Egypt today knows that you don't use your elbows the way we do. People have relatively little space or privacy, so the social bonds have to be on the side of harmonious living.

That did not mean lack of individuality, and we'll see in this book some fairly vivid personalities. But it does mean that people learned early on what society wanted, and they performed accordingly. The young, though indulged in other ways, were not given years of scuffing about the world to "find themselves" as many of us have been. If they didn't meet others' expectations, they dropped lower in the scale of things until they found their own level. We'll see this with Ramses, who sifted carefully through the first dozen of his hundred or so sons to find a proper successor. When the time came, it was not the first-born but the thirteenth who succeeded him. That was Merneptah, by then a man in his sixties.

The Gift of the Nile

The Nile's influence on Egypt ranks as the most impressive geographical relationship in the world, echoed but not equalled by similar ones in Mesopotamia (which enjoyed almost as dramatic a river-system) and elsewhere. Without the Nile, Egypt as the ancients knew it could not have existed and the development of western civilization would surely have been retarded.

To utilize the Nile flood, Egyptians needed irrigation. In most of the Nile Valley, one could (and can) stand with one foot on fertile soil and the other in the sand. When the annual inundation dropped below the norm--what they called "a bad Nile"--people literally starved. They couldn't make it up through rainfall, because outside the Delta there wasn't any, to speak of. Upper Egypt could go for years on end without a drop of rain. That left the vivid colors on ancient temples (especially Medinet Habu, by Ramses III), but it did not allow for crop-cycles apart from what the river bestowed. Ingenious methods of measuring let the authorities know what kind of crop-year to expect. Far upriver, a device called a "Nilometer" told them how deep the flood-waters would be. This information predicted how far inland they could spread the water and silt, through the canal system.

So, the Nile promoted irrigation, canals, and measuring. It also meant surveyors, land records, and boundaries. Boundaries were of prime importance. Ramses II, on the first inspection trip of his reign, found disarray in Abydos, where his father had planned and begun an extensive complex. He ascribed it partly to boundary troubles. He says, "The products of the fields were not collected, since their boundaries were not marked on the land." (See Kitchen, pp. 44-45)

LIFE IN ANCIENT EGYPT

In Ancient Egypt trained monkeys helped to harvest figs from the sycamore tree.

"Land is wealth" in Egypt as elsewhere, and more than in most places. The distribution of land among the main holders began with pharaoh himself, who theoretically owned the entire country. He could bestow land virtually forever, especially in the service of its original and perpetual owners, the gods. Hence the enormous and wealthy temple-estates, which supported priests, farmers, and villagers by the thousand. Below these two lay several tiers of owners. Ramses II redistributed land in all directions, but he followed a pattern set centuries before.

The Nile also meant technology. Ingenious water-lifting devices insured that the fellahin got the water up out of its channel and onto their crops. Even today, two of the oldest forms remain in use because they're cheaper than using motors. The most primitive, the *shaduf,* is a counterweight system that easily lifts water by offsetting its weight. We find this thing pictured on the walls of ancient tombs, and we see it in use now. It is NOT labor-efficient, but one element Egypt always had in abundance was its workers.

The other device requires more capital. They call it the *sekuia,* and one has to have an ox. It paces in circles and has only a dim idea where it's going. The ox turns a paddle wheel and THAT lifts the water. For motive power they need fodder at one end of the ox and a kid with a stick at the other.

The Nile also meant writing, records, registry offices, and a highly accurate calendar. They required a bureaucracy, a central administration, and subdivisions of their long, narrow country. Egyptians used, in their completed system, some 42 major districts called *Nomes.* Herein lay a source of stability, since local government could be exercised through them. Occasionally in its long history Egypt saw these sub-rulers out of control, but relatively seldom.

Flowers of Ancient Egypt
anemone, rose, aloe, chrysanthemum, lily, lotus

The Nile made possible the communities and the cities. It also provided a transportation system for bringing produce from one part of the country to the others. Ultimately, Egyptians could manage enormous loads on their Nile barges. We know that Ramses II brought in statues and obelisks that way which weighed up to a thousand tons.

It is no surprise that the Egyptians considered the Nile a god; in one text Ramses calls it his father. They regarded the Nile as a kind of norm for a higher civilization. We'll see a predecessor of Ramses complaining that the Euphrates River "flows the wrong way." To them, all proper rivers ought to flow north, even though few do.

Prehistoric Egypt

All of these factors gave Egypt three prerequisites for early development: a reliable environment, a stable climate, and geographical unity. Centering on the Nile Valley and the Nile Delta, with some of the world's fiercest deserts on two sides, the highlands of Africa on the third, and the Mediterranean to the north, the country could bask in its eternal sun undisturbed.

Foreigners who wished to settle or invade could creep into the country at the two corners of the Delta--Libyans from the west and Semites from the northeast. They could try to sail up the seven mouths of the Nile into the Delta. Or, they could come down the Nile from Africa and trade with Egyptians at the outpost called Suan (a word which means "market" and gives us the current place-name, Aswan, where the high dam is).

The archaeology of prehistoric Egypt shows that essentially this pattern prevailed from early Palaeolithic times onward: early flints on

the highlands, and tribes filtering in. We hear of quite mysterious peoples, the Gerzeans, the Amratians, both in the Neqada culture. We have information on them, but no documents. Hence, "prehistoric."

Hamitic invaders, akin to the modern Berbers, moved into Egypt by about 6 000 B.C. Nilotic populations followed, from the same stock as the modern inhabitants of Sudan. Semites filtered in from the north early on, and all these peoples settled down to form a country rich in ethnic origins.

Much of this is extremely obscure to us now, the three thousand years before 3100 B.C. It's prehistoric, with no direct records, but it does have mythic traditions that were picked up in Egyptian literature and religion, and it has left its archaeological traces. The only portion of this vast subject that enters a study of Ramses is what remained of it in the traditions he followed, especially religious ones.

Some religious documents demonstrate how far back Egyptians would reach into the past. For instance, the Shabaka Stone in the British Museum dates from about 700 B.C., but it derives from an original written not long after 3 000 B.C. Many religions can regard a religious text as "current" after 2,300 years this way, but Egyptians went further and considered even commentaries or minor documents as valid for millenia. (See J.B. Pritchard, *Ancient Near Eastern Texts Relating to the Old Testament,* ed. 2, Princeton, 1955, pp. 4-5.)

Similarly, a listing of the priests of Ptah preserves the names of no fewer than 60 men, each the son of the priest before, serving continuously for 1,350 years, from the Eleventh Dynasty right on through the time of Ramses to the Twentieth. We'll see that Ramses cultivated the priesthoods carefully. He even folded the names of gods

11

like Ptah and Amun and Seth into the nomenclature of his own family, and got his sons into the priesthoods.

So much for the prehistoric period and the overtones it left behind. Religion is mankind's most conservative institution, and Egyptians rank among the most conservative people ever. We can imagine the obscure influences, unsuspected now, that might have had Ramses jerking like a puppet when he made his ceremonious daily rounds. He saw gods everywhere and became the most active pharaoh in history for endowing cults or temples.

The Predynastic Period
(before 3100 B.C.)

Another aspect of prehistory that descended to Ramses was the continuity of his own office. Egyptians had a calendar very early, probably by 3100 B.C. (But not 4241, as previously thought: W.C. Hayes in *CAH* I, 1, Ch. vi.) They were obsessed with continuity. We have endless lists of their kings, highly valuable information: accounts of who ruled, precisely how long, and what events occured.

This makes a "relative chronology"--the date in their terms. Some ancient accounts mention astronomical events--comets and eclipses-- which can be dated firmly to provide an "absolute chronology," convertible into our terms (how long before the present, or since Christ lived).

We'll see later that Ramses used some of his predecessors as specific models. We have a remarkable relief at Abydos showing Ramses and his father with "the Canon of Kings"--76 royal ancestors, honored by their royal names enclosed in cartouches! They reach far back into this earliest period of Egyptian history. As I'll declare over and over, the

past stayed alive to the Ramessids, and their behavior followed lore long since lost to us.

It's true that Ramses especially admired three kings who ruled after the Old Kingdom: Sesostris III, Tuthmose III, and Amenhotep III. But he was also aware of the dim past, before the unification of Egypt about 3100 B.C., when confederacies dominated the countryside, called by such names as the Lapwings or the Nine Bows. The existence of a high office similar to that of the later pharaoh supplied known rulers with extraordinary names like the Bee, the Vulture, the Cobra, the Reed. (Generally on this period: E. Baumgartel in *CAH* I, 1, Ch. ix of the third edition, with her two volumes, *The Cultures of Prehistoric Egypt,* Oxford 1955, 1960. Further bibliography: *CAH,* ibid., pp. 654-657. W.C. Hayes, *Most Ancient Egypt,* Chicago 1965.)

At the very end of the period, kings appeared who have left personal items we can still tell were theirs, and in fact these are historical documents. A mace-head, belonging to SCORPION, names him right on it. His successor, NARMER, left a palette. It shows him wearing the white crown of Upper Egypt, and trying to conquer Lower Egypt for the god Horus. (Ramses later particularly favored Horus too, partly for the antiquity of this tradition.)

The palette shows Narmer successful in Lower Egypt, and now also wearing its red crown. From then on, Egypt could be united, calling itself "the Two Lands." The pharaoh symbolized this by wearing a combination of both crowns.

The "First Dynasties" Period
(c. 3100-2700 B.C.)

The "Protodynastic Period" (Dynasties I and II) followed the unification of Egypt, and preceded the age of the pyramids. (On their date: Hayes, *CAH* I, 1, Ch. vi.) To Ramses, the greatest moment in Egyptian history before his own birth would be the unification, traditionally accomplished by *Menes,* successor of Narmer--if he was not in fact the same man.

Centuries later, the Greeks knew Menes well, because he achieved a permanent union. It was symbolized by the double crown so that none could forget. This used the red, flat crown of the North (Lower Egypt), upon which it mounted the white, conical crown of Upper Egypt. Further signs were depiction of the papyrus, symbol of Upper Egypt, and the lotus, for Lower. (For these first kings: W.B. Emery, *Archaic Egypt* Penguin 1961). I.E.S. Edwards in *CAH* I, 2, Ch. xi.)

The capital, Memphis, or *Men-ufer,* also termed the town of the "White Wall," apparently echoed the name of Menes. Ironically, the most extensive remains there now belong to Ramses. We know that he poked around trying to bring the remote period alive, and he says himself that one of his first acts was to restore "the cenotaphs of the first kings," whom he calls "my ancestors." (See the Montreal catalogue, introduction.) Whether or not he knew of the brick tomb of Menes, it did exist, and has been rediscovered with other records. A gold apparel-fragment also names him.

We have now evidence of a highly-organized state: crystal, alabaster, gold, ivory, copper furniture; "professional" art. (For instance, the celebrated geese of Meidum used on a UNICEF Christmas card are as

old as the Great Pyramid, showing a developed style already.) Trade contacts with the Aegean began as early as 3000 B.C.

The famous Egyptian obsession with tombs went back to the beginning; it was the norm, by the days of Ramses, to begin one's tomb at the very outset of his reign.

Many tombs had been looted by the days of Ramses. One of the earliest tombs to suffer this fate, Zer's, had been mistaken for that of Osiris, to whom Ramses was especially devoted. The tomb was *buried* under offerings, some no doubt by Ramses.

The political reoganization by Menes succeeded partly because he based it on the ancient divisions, the Nomes. Ramses understood this "Protodynastic Period" well enough to dedicate his reign to perpetuating the unity of Egypt. The struggle to unify "The Two Lands" had become a faded memory, lost behind the shadow of the pyramid age, but Ramses peered intently back toward it and resolved to renew the great achievement of Menes.

The Great Tomb Tradition

When Ramses created his original tomb and those for some wives and daughters as "world-class" structures of their type, he followed a tradition over two thousand years old by his time. Early in the Old Kingdom, nobles and pharaohs tried to preserve their mortal remains.

They hit on a device called now the *Mastaba,* the Arabic word for "bench." At first, these were pits with mud-brick superstructures. By the Fourth Dynasty they employed stone; by the Sixth Dynasty there's one with *thirty* columned halls and chambers.

15

There's a woman in Chicago at the Oriental Institute who died about 3000 B.C. and was never properly mummified. She was buried casually in the sand, and it did its work. She's so perfectly preserved after 5,000 years that her family would know her. Her case is far from unique, and can be paralleled in Peru, near Mesa Verde, and elsewhere.

Now, you put people in mastabas, and you're undoing the Hot-Sand Factor. The priests come with their offerings of food for a century or so, and then somebody looks inside, horrified to discover that preservation has decidedly not occurred. Obviously, the technique needs refining.

So, they tried another. What about a massive stone structure with four sloping sides to counteract the hollowing effect of the wind? The idea of pyramids caught on.

A recent theory, based on studies out in the desert, holds that the pyramid shape is a "natural" one. It deflects the sand. The winds and the sand they carry are deadly to most shapes. One can see rectilinear forms scooped out like bars of soap, but pyramid-shaped hills just get smoother. Egyptians knew the desert, and took their cue.

There's another benefit. That massive stone superstructure a pyramid has will pass on to the pharaoh inside the hot, dry air better than a mud mastaba will, and when the body lies 200 feet in the air as that of Cheops did, there's certainly no ground-moisture.

Anyway, for better or worse, scores of pyramids went up in the Nile Valley, and of course Ramses later saw them, as we still can. To understand them, we must ponder the Old Kingdom.

The Old Kingdom

(2700-2200 B.C.)

One arrangement of the successive ruling houses of Egypt--the "Dynasties" (from a Greek word for "ruling")--groups the Third to the Sixth Dynasties as the "Old Kingdom." Looking back on their own history, later Egyptians saw in this period a certain coherence. We can agree, noting especially the stability of the kingdom then. Long reigns and great monuments bespeak a successful monarchy, as once pointed out by Sir Alan Gardiner in his *Egypt of the Pharaohs* (Oxford 1961). The period saw Egyptians create the most awesome buildings in history, the pyramids; this alone would demonstrate the country's greatness at the time. Only late in the Sixth Dynasty ensued the troubled period when a late chronicler, Manetho, said that many kings ruled, for seventy days apiece. (W.S. Smith in *CAH* I, 2, Ch. xiv; on the chronology, W.C. Hayes, ibid., I, 1, Ch. 6. Baines and Malek, 32-35, regard the Old Kingdom as beginning with the Fourth Dynasty.)

The Old Kingdom stands yet as one of the most colorful and exciting periods of human history. An enlightened monarch ruled with theoretically absolute power, limited only by tradition and by conceptions of justice as overseen by the gods. He (or, in one case, she) ruled a vigorous and enthusiastic bureaucracy, well controlled by learned officials, carefully structured to form a pyramid of authority reaching back up to the pharaoh.

This superb administration looked after a complex irrigation system on which the country depended. Under central control, a lively international commerce was carried on with Nubia to the south and the Levant to the northeast. The gradual enrichment of Egypt had begun, without which no such grand conception as a pyramid could

have been carried out. Ramses also appreciated the *monumentality* of pyramids, but wisely chose a different way of handling both immortality and architectural statement.

At least in these early centuries of the Old Kingdom, Egyptians considered that the entire society had a stake in the pharaoh's immortality. Laboring for him, they worked also for themselves. Belief and compulsion combined to keep 100,000 men building the Great Pyramid for 20 years, if we can believe the account given to Herodotus two thousand years later.

The pyramids sprang from elements characteristic of the Old Kingdom, and no doubt Ramses wished to revive some of these, especially after the dismal reign of Akhnaton.

The Pyramids

When Napoleon visited Egypt and pronounced that "Forty centuries look down upon us," he must have been thinking of the pyramids. The most massive stone buildings ever created need no praise. They have astonished mankind since the day they arose, and still stand unsurpassed. So enormous are they, yet so refined in detail and technical accomplishment, that some can explain them only by seeing gods in chariots descend to build them.

We have easily available accounts by scholars who have long specialized in pyramids. The most accessible are the Penguin by I.E.S. Edwards, *The Pyramids of Egypt* (1947, revised 1961 and reisssued often), and Ahmed Fakhry's *The Pyramids* (Chicago 1961; ed. 2, 1969).

Northwind Picture Archives

PYRAMID

The Step-Pyramid at Saqqara

Perhaps inspired by the Mesopotamian Ziggurats, Egyptians developed a stone version of the multi-stepped platform. They called this version *Pyramid,* or in their terms, *per-em-us.* The first pharaoh to attempt this form was *Zoser,* the second king of the Third Dynasty, who began to rule not long after 2650 B.C. His building began as a mastaba, but we've seen the problems these tombs could create, the main one being failure to preserve the body, its main purpose, after all.

In the final version, Zoser achieved the world's first great stone building, which still stands. It rose in six stages to a height of just over 200 feet, something like fourteen stories in an assymmetrical base of about 400 by 350 feet. A solid, box-like core of local stone secured it, they hoped forever. As with the later pyramids, a casing of Tura limestone enveloped the building, which gleamed awesomely in the ever-present sun and struck the groundlings mute with astonishment. The multiple revisions show his architects feeling their way to the new form, and the use of small blocks demonstrate their inexperience with stone.

The site chosen could hardly have been better, the area now called Saqqara, not far from ancient Memphis (near modern Cairo). Nearby the Nile Valley ends as the river flows north into its several mouths which diverge in the Delta. Egypt proper lies south, with its other great city, Thebes, some 400 miles away.

The pyramid stood in the desert well away from the Nile but visible to all who toiled on its banks. Its elevation contributed to the impressiveness created by its size, and the massive complex which surrounded it ranked in some minds with the pyramid itself. An echo

of Memphis also resided there, as if the pharaoh had created a ghostly version of his city in which to rest and serve his people for eternity.

Ramses was, of course, fully aware of the great complex, visible from the Great Pyramid, which he and his son, Khaemwaset, worked to restore. A Ramessid chapel from Saqqara, built in the shadow of this complex, depicts and names three seated kings of the Third Dynasty. (*CAH* I, 2, p. 150.) Ramses built no pyramids, but the idea of an integrated complex could have come to him here and inspired such unifying constructions as his wall around the temples at Karnak.

Ramses understood the honor given to Zoser's architect, Imhotep. Graffiti from over a thousand years later honor this man, as Ramses did his own architects, whose statues have survived. This profession placed its successful practitioners high in the human pyramid.

The Step-Pyramid will grace our newscasts for generations to come. The quality of its internal construction, its beautiful external columns, the enticing shafts as much as 90 feet deep still filled with ancient rubble and pottery, the pink granite tomb chamber, the alabaster coffins, the child remains, the "stolen" vases from the First and Second Dynasties, the wooden platforms perhaps used by ancient tomb-robbers, the thousands of artifacts known and visible--these are all materials for future interest.

Meidum

At *Meidum,* some thirty miles upstream from Saqqara, lies a transitional building, by the first pharaoh of the Fourth Dynasty, Sneferu. With relative suddenness, the pyramid had achieved something of its fully developed scale, for now we have a massive

building 473 feet square. Still not the size pyramids would achieve, but for a solid stone building this was, down to that date, unparalleled.

Investigations begun by Petrie in 1891 and carried on by others since reveal a possible start as a mastaba or small step-pyramid, all concealed in the present building. The workmen's sketches show that they experimented with two-step, three-step, and four-step pyramids. This building's core is in fact a seven-step pyramid.

The procedure followed entailed construction of seven successive towers, each of which expanded the previous one. Six thick coatings of masonry helped bind the structure. The center tower rises highest, with the height diminishing progressively downward. The inclines are extraordinarily steep at 75 degrees; since these are not bonded, the inward tilt must serve as the main force preserving the building's integrity.

The final raising added some 45 feet to the building, a three-storey rise which resulted in an eight-step core. The final transformation then entailed packing the steps with local stone to create the now-familiar angle of a "true" pyramid, then creating a smooth Tura limestone casing. *Voila!* An apparently true pyramid built atop a much-revised step pyramid.

As an experiment, this came off fairly well, and the lower half remains mostly intact, covered by sand for thousands of years. A sloping shaft angles down to a tomb-chamber entered in 1882.

The surrounding buildings became the later standard for a pyramid-complex: a subsidiary pyramid, a mortuary temple, a causeway, and a valley building near the Nile, with a canal leading to the precious water itself.

Meidum apparently stood unfinished, for two stelae found there exhibit blank faces where we expect reference to the king. In addition, some temple courses have not been dressed.

Why do scholars think the building Sneferu's? Though the traditions are unreliable, graffiti from the Sixth Dynasty onward mention him. Tourists contributed their own sentiments down into the Eighteenth Dynasty, fourteen centuries later. One, in the reign of Tuthmose III about 1475 B.C., after identifying himself as the former scribe of Tuthmose I, says, "I...came to see the beautiful temple of King Sneferu (and) found it as though heaven were within it and the sun rising in it."

The Pyramids at Dahshur

Sneferu also created the first true pyramid, back up near Memphis, about two miles south of the city. He planned a true pyramid from the ground up, as it were, and failed to achieve it; nearby, he succeeded. The two pyramids are known as the "Bent Pyramid" and, less poetically, the "Northern Stone Pyramid at Dahshur."

The Bent Pyramid bears that curious name because of a strange flattening. Even from a distance, one can see that the Bent Pyramid has an irregular slope. The workers began well enough, with an angle at the base of 54 degrees, close to the later standard. However, about halfway up the outer casing changes abruptly to 43 degrees and slopes determinedly on up to the apex.

Certain signs may explain this little mystery. Stonework in the upper half appears less meticulous than before. The flatter angle has cut down the building's volume considerably over what it would have been had the 54-degree slope been maintained. The pyramid will now

be shorter than it would have been otherwise, but of course it will not take as long to build. This latter may be the clue that Sneferu had died during construction, or expected to, or could not maintain the pace of his three pyramids without this change.

Its base covers 620 feet on a side, and the building is a square. Like later pyramids, it is oriented to the four cardinal points of the compass, not as well as those at Gizeh, but its builders had the right idea.

Of all the greater pyramids, this counts as the best preserved, since much of the Tura casing remains in place. The building's construction appears even more "solid" than the norm for these great structures, because its stones incline in, angled downward toward the center. It is as if the potential flaw in the pyramid at Meidum had been detected and was here being reversed, yielding a far stronger mass. The inward tilt also meant an outside easier to dress for the blocks composing its outer face, since its slope more closely approached theirs.

Well did this pyramid deserve its proud title, "Sneferu gleams." Another unparalleled feature is double entrances. One sits as usual in the north face, angling at 25 degrees downward for some 240 feet. It reaches a chamber 41 feet high, and *corbelled*--the technique by which each course of stone in a vault projects inward more than the one below it did. This can gradually roof a large area with a self-supporting arch or vault or even dome. It was to figure in great buildings for centuries, and its use on such a scale perhaps begin here.

It gives onto another chamber, cone-shaped and 57 feet high. Both of these stand under the pyramid, the top of the second one flush with its base. A third chamber in the body of the pyramid, also cone-shaped and 42 feet high, completes this astonishing construction. Whether Ramses saw these rooms is questionable; the pyramid's entrances were

sealed under the casing, but pyramids were breached in antiquity, and his restless inspectors doubtless knew ways to get in.

The alternate entrance begins on the west, and leads by a long descending passage to the third chamber, the one in the body of the pyramid. Thick cedar bolstering still exists here, and what looks like plaster refilling of cracks. Did the building move or settle during construction? On the other hand, this might have figured in supporting the heavy sarcophagus on its journey inward.

Other features found in the pyramid include to bar the corridors, rubble fill, and even an escape passage for the last workmen in the building, as found also in the Great Pyramid. Nearby, a relief helps identify the building as by Sneferu, just like its neighbor.

The Northern Stone Pyramid at Dahshur

Here at last stands the earliest completed true pyramid, conceived as one and carried through appropriately. At 719 feet on each of its square sides, it stands second in size only to the Great Pyramid at Gizeh.

What strikes the eye here is not the change of angle as with its bent sister, but the flatness of angle--43 degrees, about the same as the upper half of the Bent. This is much flatter than the norm for other pyramids, and striking now by comparison, but when the building was new no "standard" yet existed.

Like the Bent, this pyramid boasts three chambers, but all stand within its body. Two high corbelled rectangular chambers lead to a third corbel 50 feet high.

25

Outside, the paraphernalia of a pyramid surround it, including mastabas for his courtiers. One relief shows females bearing offerings symbolizing Sneferu's estates as he began his great journey in comfort.

There is little difficulty in indentifying the pharaoh responsible for this pyramid. Sneferu's Horus name, one of the series of throne-names a pharaoh took, was written in ochre on a block in the building.

An inscription discovered in 1905 refers to "the two pyramids of Sneferu." That probably refers to these two at Dahshur, though a reference to Meidum cannot be rejected. If all three are securely his, attempts may be justified to ascertain the order of construction, and some dated blocks appear to show that Meidum and Dahshur North were simultaneous, with the Bent somewhat later, an attempt to build a "true" pyramid at 53 degrees which failed. Such questions for so major a turning-point in the history of architecture show the precarious state of our knowledge. The main questions are not always the ones for which we have the answers.

The Pyramids at Gizeh

To understand Ramses, we must examine what next occured. Here lies the great achievements in history, one he simultaneously admired and emulated, since he could not imitate.

Cheops (Khufu, in Egyptian), son of Sneferu, has left a surprisingly dim echo in history, apart from his building. But it's enough. A few reliefs of him exist, some mining records, a tiny ivory statue in Cairo, and legends. He repeated and expanded his father's "discovery" of the "true" pyramid. He chose an area on the plateau west of the modern

26

PYRAMID

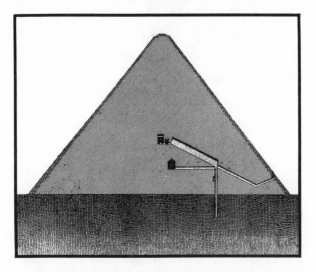

CROSS-SECTION SHOWING TOMB

town of Gizeh, across the Nile from Memphis, about 15 miles south of Cairo. This area lies on the eastern edge of the desert, just beyond the cultivated lushness of the Nile Valley. About four miles further south can be seen the Step-Pyramid at Saqqara, where it all began.

The Great Pyramid

Cheops labored some twenty years on this building. He fashioned the greatest of the genre, big enough to hold the cathedrals of Milan, Florence, St. Peter's in Rome, St. Paul's in London, and Westminster Abbey--all at once.

The word "enormous" should apply nowhere but here, reserved to describe the product of more than two million blocks, each from two to fifteen tons in weight, and within 1/100 of an inch of being a true square. The excellent workmanship continues even in parts of the building designed to remain forever unseen.

The base sets square, 755 feet on each side. That's two football fields, endzones, and change--whether NFL or the larger Canadian stadium. The corners describe near--perfect right angles, with a maximum error of 3 minutes, but a minimum of only two *seconds*. That gives a mean error from a perfect square of just 7/10 of an inch. We get by with larger margins on virtually everything built today.

The pyramid originally reared up some 481 feet, of which the top 31 are now lost. A few seconds with the slide rule will tell you that these dimensions give an area of thirteen acres for it to set upon.

The pyramid is oriented to the cardinal points of the compass, within a range of two to five minutes of angle, or 1/20 of one degree of

true north. How they did that without a magnetic compass baffles modern inquiry.

When Ramses pondered the details of this project, he learned a great deal. Some 100,000 men, organized in work-gangs as the quarry-marks demonstrate, labored in three-month shifts for twenty years. Whatever the details, he could see here that even the most enormous project could be accomplished if set up properly and adequately manned. His appetite for great buildings and foreign wars alike here meshed: fight the wars to obtain the captives to build the monuments.

Ramses, like Cheops, required a vehicle for the afterlife. His father, Seti I, had been much concerned about this, and both agreed that a pyramid could not suffice, since it would not preserve them and would undoubtedly prove too expensive. Hence their sumptuous tombs, with their ample resources going otherwise to great public temples.

The Great Sphinx

Ramses also toyed with another form for which local inspiration was available at Gizeh. Near the Great Pyramid, and closer still to that of Chephren (Khafre), crouches one of the compelling figures of all time, the lion with the head of the sun-god Aton. Given a body 240 feet long and a face about thirteen feet across rearing up 66 feet above your own, this animal commands your attention.

It wears the royal head-dress, complete with the uraeus cobra. Ramses was fascinated, and here we need no guess as to his attitude. Time after time, he poses as a sphinx himself. An enormous version lies as practically all that remains of Memphis. This triumph over death, and renewal of the Nile flood, came to him as a sufficient double

LARGE SCALE CONSTRUCTIONS FROM ANCIENT EGYPT
NOTICE SIZE OF HUMAN FIGURES

attraction to dress this way and assume a lion's body. That age-old identification with the sun attracted the sun-pharaoh irresistibly. (Montreal catalogue, no. 65)

The "Lesson" of the Pyramids

When Ramses pondered pyramids, he must first have thought about the Great Pyramid and the two others at Giza, with the early one at Saqqara visible from them. This line they formed along the desert edge was not accidental. *Sun* is the key. The rising sun touches their tips, as it does too for obelisks. Statues like the Colossi of Memnon (two 450-ton monsters at Thebes) are so positioned as to "greet" the dawn. One of them used to "squeal" as the sun warmed a flaw in the rock inside it, thus bestowing the fantods on bystanders. Ramses greatly admired these, built by his hero, Amenhotep III.

Sun in the form of the god Re was central to Egyptian beliefs, and a matter of special attention, since both end with Ra's name: UsimaRE SetepenRE. His family came from a region also special to Re (Ra), as we'll see later.

Pyramids were important in this regard. In declining to attempt one, Ramses did not miss their significance. He tried to attain the same ends by different means. Pyramids existed as tombs, yes, but why so elaborate? It wasn't only to protect pharaoh's mummy. In fact, often it did not. Many pyramids were breached in antiquity. What did they accomplish? Texts which have descended to us provide clues.

For instance, the word itself. We use a later Greek form, *pyramis,* but the original was *per-em-us,* a term used in mathematical texts for

the *height* of the pyramid. In other words, the entire thing was named after its height, which was their real interest in it. Why?

We have another clue from the angle most pyramids described with the ground, usually about 52 degrees. If we see one at sunrise, looking eastward from the desert, or at sunset, looking westward from the Nile Valley, we're struck by the visual proximity of the angle of the sun's rays to the angle of the sides of the pyramid, as if the rays of the sun are sliding down the side of the pyramid, or are even in some mysterious way identical with it.

The ancient sheathing of white Tura limestone that covered the pyramids made this an especially compelling sight, since the whole thing gleamed. Part of that layer remains in place on the middle pyramid at Gizeh, the one for Chephren.

How to explain it? In 1880, and in bits and pieces since, what scholars call "the Pyramid Texts" were discovered, usually on the walls of tombs. These are spells for pharaoh's use, going back at least to the pyramid of Unas in the Fifth Dynasty.

Spell 508 addresses the sun, saying "I use thy rays as a ramp when I mount." Spell 523 says to the pharaoh, "Heaven has strengthened for thee the rays, so that you can lift yourself to heaven." In other words, the pyramid is a *machine,* a lifting device for the spirit of the dead pharaoh. Like so many things Egyptian, it is beautiful asthetically, but its true purpose was practical.

It is to endure forever, so it's granite. The pharaoh will take journeys from it, so he gets a solar boat, of which examples have been found in fine working condition, including one of the boats for Cheops, the world's oldest cedar boat. We have yachtsmen who trust their lives every weekend to boats not as stable as those things still are.

The idea that pharaoh journeys *up* is embedded right in the language. A word which occurs in many pyramid-part names is 'r, which you find also in *Ramses,* of course, by way of his identification with Ra. That's the verb meaning "to ascend," and when you want to be sure people know that's what you mean, you add what's called a "determinative"--a little descriptive picture. In this case it's a tiny step-pyramid, perfectly appropriate and understandable.

Spell 267 in fact says, "a staircase to heaven is laid for the pharaoh, so that he can climb up thereby." The step-pyramids look like Mesopotamian Ziggurats, which had the same purpose, letting a king or a maiden rise to the level where the gods would come down.

What has this to do with the revelation about Ramses not building his own pyramid? He pondered the purpose of the pyramid, which was to let pharaoh ride the solar boat around the sky each night for the good of the people.

Ramses was searching for an alternative which would reap the same benefits. He found one. Why not *identify* himself with the sun god here below, and get his family involved in the cults, then just concentrate on preserving his body? That way, he'd benefit his people before death, since he *was* the sun-god, and later there'd be no need of the sun trying to find him every evening in his tomb, since he'd find himself. He could then set forth to collect the others.

It was more complex than that, as we'll see, but not far from that. Ramses took care to stress this theme during his magnificent building program, and it's one reason he so loved gold. Egyptians always did.

They liked gold because it shone like the sun, with the same color, and because it does not decay like other metals, or react with soil. Ramses always promoted the opening of new gold mines. In one

famous story the vizier found water where others had failed for centuries, and that opened up the gold-bearing desert of Akuyati.

Ramses valued gold, because it reminded him of the sun, which he wanted to identify with, so that he wouldn't need to build a pyramid. He saved a fortune, and didn't have to wait twenty years to see his own building.

The Instinct for Empire

It's not surprising that Ramses looked with longing back to the great age of Cheops and the pyramids. As Sir Alan Gardiner once remarked, "If its five great pyramids were all that the *Fourth Dynasty* had to show by way of accomplishment, these would still have to be viewed as a manifestation of purposeful power and technical genius unsurpassed in any age or clime." (*Egypt of the Pharaohs,* Oxford 1961, p. 76.)

So, we've united Egypt, set up its pharaoh, discerned in its mastabas and pyramids the inspiration for Ramses and his temples and his obsession with gold. Several points remain: How did the Egyptians acquire the instinct for empire, on which Ramses grew so great? Was it there before "foreigners" (like the Hyksos in their fright-wigs) arrived to instill it? How did their office of pharaoh permit control of foreign territory? How did the marvellous Egyptian pantheon of gods, part animal and part human, justify expansion of the Two Lands?

First, empire. One rationale for expansion was conquest and the slaves it brought home to work the economy. We know Ramses by titles suggesting greatness, and he intended that. We also know him as the pharaoh of the Jewish Exodus, and we'll see the evidence for that later. (It's interesting that the name of Moses would be written in

Egyptian with the same symbols as the second half of the name of Ramses was.)

Ramses' treatment of foreign slaves as distinct from native workers could be quite harsh. The complaints of Jews under Ramses ring true, and a relief at Luxor shows him with his two sons, enthusiastically whipping Moabites. There was little recourse for the slaves. However, the villagers of Deir el-Medina managed a real strike against their Ramessid employer.

It's hard to explain how Egyptians obtained such dominion under the Old Kingdom, especially late in the period. Evolutions in Mesopotamia as Sargon of Akkad encountered the Sumerians and others about 2350 B.C. must have roused echoes in Egypt. The restoration of Sumerian power under Ur-Nammu and the Third Dynasty of Ur for a century after 2100 betokened more stability than it bestowed, and turmoil lay ahead both for Mesopotamia and for Egypt.

Nevertheless, Egyptians had by now achieved one of the most remarkable civilizations ever. Egypt managed this while every group outside of Mesopotamia had illustrated comparatively less progress.

The Old Kingdom reached outward almost from the beginning, especially with vigorous commerce. Vessels 170 feet long existed by the time of Sneferu in the Fourth Dynasty. His son, Cheops, had fine solar boats alongside the Great Pyramid. Copper arrived from Sinai, and an Egyptian fortress existed already on the Isthmus of Suez--both places where Ramses had conquered again, following a tradition over a thousand years old by his time. When he took the high road east from the Delta, he followed Sneferu thirteen centuries before, after whom some of those roads were still named in his day.

Ramses spent a lot of time in Lebanon, ensuring supply-lines. Here he followed another tradition that saw the earliest known expeditions on the open seas, in search of cedar for the temple of Amun, which Ramses later did so much for.

Another theme in the reign of Ramses was Nubia, the modern Sudan and parts of Ethiopia. Nubians preferred independence. They had some little surprises in store during the centuries ahead, when the Twenty-Fifth Dynasty ruled even Egypt.

Expeditions against Nubia went back to the Old Kingdom. There could be an entire catalogue of ways Ramses echoed themes from back then. It would be analogous in our chronological system for someone to set foreign policy along lines established in 600 A.D. Not often done, but again we see that Egyptians rank among the most conservative of peoples.

The Office of Pharaoh

So we'll see in Ramses a vigorous pharaoh, active internationally, following leads set for him from the Old Kingdom. He was probably doing this even when his policies extended to the world's first extant treaty of non-aggression, forged with the Hittite Empire. It's the type of imaginative action that the Old Kingdom would have approved. Although the impulse probably came more from the Hittite side, where there was a strong tradition of peace-making, at least Ramses had the flexibility to recognize its utility and adopt it.

That contributed to world peace for decades at an important stage in the evolution of great empires: the Babylonian, the Hittite, the

Assyrian, and the Egyptian. Much had changed internationally since the Old Kingdom, but the centuries of Egyptian diplomatic activity between that time and Ramses helped prepare his foreign policy.

Now, when the Old Kingdom perfected the position of pharaoh, the most successful political office in world history if we judge by the length of time it endured, how did it build in such continuity coupled with flexibility and stability?

One clue to the original attitude lies in the name for pharaoh. That curious word has been seen by some scholars as deriving from *Per-aa*, a term meaning "the Great House."

Egyptians thought the pharaoh abode with them until he joined the gods, so he *was* the great structure himself. Other derivations try to explain the word through different terms in the Egyptian language, and one even sees the name **pro-* cognate with *proteus,* the Greek name for the original Old Man of the Sea, who could change shapes (hence our derivative 'protein'). At least to judge by the later story in which Helen of Troy's husband wrestles him in the sea off Egypt, trying to gain the occult knowledge Proteus had, the name of pharaoh could imply a higher type of knowledge--nice to have in a sovereign, as Plato knew. We don't, unfortunately, know for certain where the term came from.

Nature of the Office

An institution as solid as the great office of pharaoh takes time, but it developed over the centuries into the center of one of the tightest,

most efficient bureaucracies ever known. We tend to think of bureaucracy as a modern curse, but ancients took great pride in these things, and the records show that Egypt had a superb one, as too did ancient Crete and Mesopotamia. High organization came early to these great civilizations.

Pharaoh presided, but not alone, even for Ramses. One formula said, "Great is the pharaoh who has great counsellors." We'll see that nobody took this more seriously than Ramses did, with a circle of amazing individuals, some inherited from his father's reign, a pattern which can be detected far back in Egyptian history.

Nobles and officials did pharaoh's will, but they also formed a check on him. There was a vast reservoir of experience there, and a good pharaoh used it. Great power resided in the higher officials and priests, which was the right arrangement for such a long, narrow country. Centralized power directly controlling officials hundreds of miles upriver or down provided the right combination of authority and flexibility.

Other traditional maxims bade the pharaoh rule within strict standards of justice, and govern in company with the twelve great gods. He himself later went among them as a *neter,* that is, a god too.

Usually he enjoyed a special relationship to Re and Amun, and became a *neter nefer,* "a goodly god," or a "Great KA"--a kind of guardian spirit. *Nefer* was a most useful term, and could apply to queens as well: for instance, the famous Nefertiti, or the first Great Queen of Ramses, Nefertari.

Pharaoh ranked higher than all humans, and just below the eternal gods. He could in fact believe he was the son of a god, as Ramses called

himself son of Ptah, or Queen Hatshepsut said she was born of Amun-Ra.

When pharaoh gave his daughter in marriage to a foreign king, as when he sent an Egyptian princess to King Solomon as wife, he believed he was conferring a breath of immortality on that whole external dynasty. Hence the great care with which Egyptians arranged this type of honor. Ramses later learned to use it judiciously. The pharaoh could also be an Atum sun-god, or the god Khnum, who gave life to clay pottery and modelled it into human beings.

This idea of divine birth for pharaoh went back into the Old Kingdom. (Montet 59) Most of the funerary temples from then have perished, but one shows the vulture-goddess Nekhbet suckling a new-born pharaoh. Khnum watches, having molded the child. In other versions, Hathor is a divine wet-nurse of the newborn pharaoh.

Memphis had a role in these early myths too, and in the evolution of the pharaonic office during the Old Kingdom, but it was later supplanted by Thebes. Did Ramses think of that earlier role when he so much favored Memphis?

The pharaoh could even determine what fate his subjects met. One old text stated that "Whoever the pharaoh loves will have a pension and a tomb. Whoever opposes pharaoh has no tomb and lies unburied in the water."

Pharaoh as Hero

Ramses has been condemned as blood-thirsty or as unwise, willing to fight on for twenty years for lands his father tried to settle by treaty. But again we find him pursuing an old ideal.

Ramses greatly admired Sesostris III, a legendary conqueror of the Twelfth Dynasty in the Middle Kingdom, who lived about 600 years before him. Ramses in fact used a nickname, "Sesu," which deliberately echoed the basic name of that king, Senwosret. Sesostris once said, "A courageous man must attack. Retreat is cowardly. He who fails to go beyond his own frontier is a ------."

The text went on to say that to be a true son--another theme in Ramses' life--you had to go out and fight as your father had. Ramses had no doubt of his father's intentions in that regard, since he joined campaigns as a boy.

As to military vigor for young pharaohs, there's a stela of Amenhotep II showing that at age 18 he had become an accomplished warrior and veteran of battle. This pattern also mounted to higher antiquity. About 1960 B.C. the papyrus account of Sinuhe shows the pharaoh's oldest son personally commanding an army. Farther back still, the Old Kingdom pharaoh Pepi I of the Sixth Dynasty conducted operations apparently in the Delta; though his commander, Uni, makes no mention of having royal blood, he may have been related to the pharaonic house. (Sinuhe: J.B. Pritchard, *Ancient Near Eastern Texts Relating to the Old Testament,* Princeton 1955, pp. 18-22. Uni: J.H. Breasted, *Ancient Records of Egypt,* vol. I, Chicago 1906, p. 142 ff.)

The Coronation of Pharaoh

Another holdover from deep antiquity was the ceremony of coronation itself. The ceremony entailed presentation of the double crown representing the Two Lands. In effect, it was a double coronation.

Many have described it as a most happy time. The son and successor of Ramses, Merneptah, left a text saying, "Glorious days are here, and a new lord has appeared." Ramses IV earned sumptuous praise, where heaven and earth rejoiced, those who were hungry, thirsty, naked, in exile, or dirty all got tended to.

The Egyptians knew the value of colorful ceremony, and it accorded well with their lavishness in other of what they deemed society's great needs. A people capable of pyramids, or of temples like those erected by Amenhotep III or Ramses II, certainly required the full panoply of solemn ceremony when the highest office of the land fell vacant. In the case of Ramses, his ceremony had to keep them impressed for a reign of 67 years. No wonder pharaohs took care to invent supplementary occasions, such as the many jubilees a long-lived pharaoh would enjoy.

Ramses and the Old Kingdom

For his coronation, Ramses II chose Thebes, a favorite place since the Eighteenth Dynasty for that, and already in the Old Kingdom one of the two most important spots in Egypt. The god Amun was there and the priests wished to hold the coronation there, despite Ramses' own reservations. To be pharaoh, one had to start out at Thebes.

Just after his coronation he headed north to Abydos, another place much frequented in the Old Kingdom, where his father, Sethos I, was active too. Then Ramses resumed building a new capital city named for himself, Pi-Ramses, "House of Ramses." Here he broke with Old Kingdom tradition in one sense by diverting the capital from Thebes or Memphis, but in another he kept with the old attitude that Egypt could be governed from one of its extremities. Instead of Thebes, at the

southern end of the country, he chose the Delta, at the other.

When Ramses assumed the throne, he used a monogram showing the lily of southern Egypt joined with the papyrus plant of northern Egypt, both with the sign for "union" in hieroglyphics. This thing can be traced back to the First Dynasty, and of course it symbolized the unity of the Two Lands.

Ramses was careful to honor both Seth, god of Upper Egypt, and Horus, god of Lower Egypt. He even named some of his many children with gods' names, including these two. All traditional. Horus was especially important to any pharaoh because, of the four names the pharaoh took, the third came from this god, the so-called "Golden Horus" name.

Ramses looked back to the Old Kingdom and remembered that the longest reign in Egyptian history had occured then, when Pepi II ruled just under 100 years, the longest reign in history. Ramses ruled for 67 years. One of his successors aspired to rule as long as he had, but made only 6 years.

Ramses could look back to this long period when the art-forms achieved such marvels that they were never excelled, as for instance in the bright, unfading tomb-paintings. Nobody ever again built something like the Great Pyramid, and people admired such marvels as international commerce, ocean-going ships, a system of law and technology, high achievements in literature and theology, where the afterlife first came to depend on one's activity here. One who "passed" post-mortem examination in the presence of Anubis, Maat, and others could drink the water of paradise. But depictions often include the ominous figure of the earth-god, Geb, crouching opposite in the form of a crocodile.

LIFE IN ANCIENT EGYPT

In Ancient Egypt acrobatic dancers and musicians often entertained at parties.

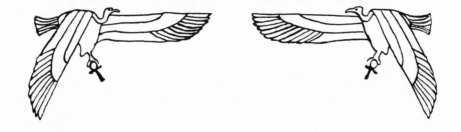

Chapter 2

Gods and Heroes
and Hyksos

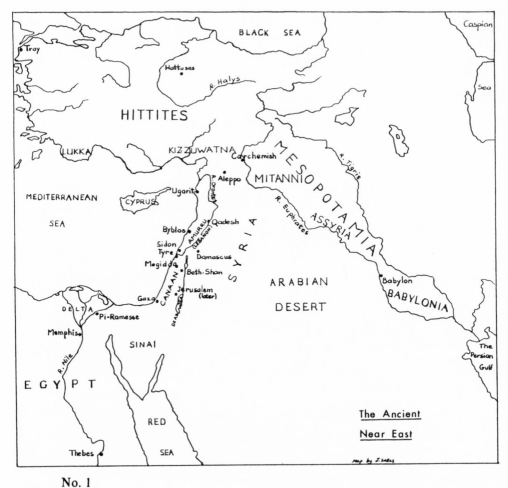

The Ancient
Near East

map by J. Saks

No. 1

Ramses and the Gods

Ramses touched base with all the gods, but several promised him more, in his view, than others did. He called himself, "the chosen of the Sun, dear to Amun and Ptah." That assured him the loyalty of their cities, Heliopolis ("city of the sun") and Thebes, home of Amun, as well as Memphis, the city of Ptah.

Ptah struck somebody like Ramses as a most useful god, patron of craftsmen and builders, the creator god later identified with Osiris and so connected with Horus, and also with the ancient Apis bull ritual. Ptah was big in three places where Ramses was too: Thebes, Abydos, and Nubia. Ramses took care to make one of his sons a priest of Ptah, and named another one for Ptah, as well as his successor, Merneptah. Greatest center of worship for Ptah was Memphis. Here it was that priests of Ptah descended in an unbroken line for some 13 centuries to his time--60 of them on one commemoration, each one a son of the priest before, each ruling for an average of over twenty years. This gave marvellous stability to that priesthood.

For Ramses, it was important to control Memphis tightly since he hoped to shift the focus of Egypt northward into the Delta, and Memphis stood right there at the head of the Delta, near where Cairo does now. It was also important to him that this priesthood had served right on through the time of the Hyksos, which he's recalling in the Stele of the Year 400. That continuity was important to him. On that same document, he tries to establish his family's pedigree, since the Nineteenth Dynasty lacked direct pharaonic descent.

To Ramses, two gods ranked higher than most. Seth, one of the nine gods of Heliopolis and god of the Tanis region of the Delta where

47

Ramses' family arose, was linked to Horus too, as the brother of Osiris. Seth was the closest of the Egyptian gods to Baal of the Semites in Syria, a region Ramses wanted to cultivate. He even went so far as to name a daughter after a Syrian god; Bint-Anath.

Ramses got his lead regarding Seth from his own father, who was the first pharaoh to use that god's name when he became Seti (or Sethos) I. People feared Seth, as god of evil and disorder, of war and storm and of the desert. He was also god of the animals of the desert, especially those with red fur. As the god of things colored red, he was of use to sun-pharaohs and had been named in the royal titles for thousands of years. On becoming queen, a woman is "one who sees her Horus and her Seth," the brothers. Seth was of especial interest to Ramses, who sported quite a shock of red hair, still visible on the mummy, though a touch faded. When the mummy was taken to Paris for treatment against a fungus ten years ago, an examination showed deep red roots to his hair.

Ramses was careful to call Seth "the father of his fathers" and make him an ancestor in that way; he didn't dare go all the way and claim to be son of him, as he did of the sun-god. Still, he was careful to follow his father's lead, who had made a special trip to Avaris to honor Seth and his importance to Hyksos times. So we come back again to the Stele of Year 400, honoring that period.

Another reason for that stele was an apparent conjunction about the time of the birth of Ramses between the two facets of the Egyptian calendar, the solar and the "Sothic." They knew about the extra 1/4 day in the year, and in their regular calendar they allowed for it. But just to be sure they weren't following some mistake by the gods, they also used a calendar omitting the quarter-day. Every 1,461 years, the

two calendars would catch up and synchronize. This seems to have happened for Ramses or his family around 1320 B.C. At least, so it appeared at the time.

Sun and Moon

The relation of Ramses to the sun as well as to Amun and Re reached far into the past for its basic materials, but it also looked to the present. The sun melts the snows of Ethiopia and their water moves down the Nile to the crops. The sun then provides unfailing nourishment for the plants, and they for the people. A marvellous system, and it seldom failed.

The variable was not the sun, as it might be in cloudy lands, but the water. If they had a "low Nile," they must brace for hardship, even famine. This occurred right through Egyptian history. Even near the end, Cleopatra and her brother had once to issue a rescript forbidding the grain merchants from diverting their produce to the areas of higher price; the Ptolemies demanded that it come to Alexandria first, under heavy penalties.

Egyptians regarded the sun and moon together as the two eyes of god. The left eye, the moon, receives the light of the right eye, the sun, and gives it back. The god *Thoth* looked after the moon, and was often symbolized by the form of a baboon.

Ramses has a small sun-and-moon chapel at Abu Simbel. Part of it travels with his Exhibit, including some of the baboons he carefully arranged there to gather in the sun's disk on the altar-top before them, and reflect it via the moon.

In mythology, these four baboons represented the four male spirits

of Hermopolis who were said to have fathered the sun. One scribe named after Ramses, Ramsesnakht, who served under Ramses IV, has his statue topped with a little baboon of Thoth. (Montreal no. 7.)

Ramses proceeded meticulously in the construction of the chapel. Some of the fine points have only lately been worked out by scholars. For instance, the solar cult and liturgy already over 2,000 years old by the time of Ramses can now be reconstructed because of the superb preservation of his little chapel at Abu Simbel which was rediscovered in 1909. (See Montreal no. 21.)

Like an architect Ramses admired (Amenhotep-Huy), Ramses would say, "I did not copy what had been done," but in every case, his work began from initiatives taken by his father or his predecessors. The campaigns in Syria, Nubia, Libya; the new capital city; the great buildings; the international relations; the foreign wives; the treatment of slaves; the religious activities--in all these he didn't do what had not been done before, he just did it better.

His relation to the beginnings of Egypt under Narmer and Menes, to the Old Kingdom conquerors, to the pyramid builders, and to the religious thinkers of two thousand years before remained close.

Thus the Old Kingdom and its various influences on Ramses.

The First Intermediate Period
(c. 2200-2000 B.C.)

The First Intermediate Period contained Dynasties VII to X. The Old Kingdom was collapsing then after 600 years.

Ramses knew that these shadowy dynasties were run by nobles

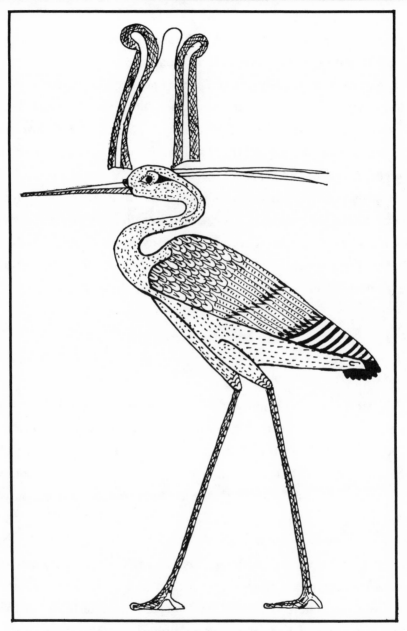

BENNU THE SACRED HERON
SYMBOL OF THE SOUL OF OSIRIS

51

trying to set up oligarchies. These nobles left no impressive pyramids, no major monuments, no records on Sinai.

Kings ruling "for seventy days" each cannot accomplish great tasks. That hyperbole by a later chronicler does cut to the essence of these two hundred years, for Egypt: the greatness paused. So far as we can tell, Egypt merely hung on to what it had accomplished in the Old Kingdom, and waited for new vigor.

Hindsight can be dangerous when it leads to negative conclusions about so long a period of time, and future discoveries may force revisions. Nevertheless, it seems safe to say that for major models, Ramses probably skipped over this period and focused on the period of renewed stability now known as the Middle Kingdom.

The Middle Kingdom
(c. 2000-1786 B.C.)

This period can be said to have begun before the end of the First Intermediate Period, in that the Eleventh Dynasty, which inaugurated it, began to exist as early as about 2130 B.C. The Tenth Dynasty, with which the end of that period is usually associated, did not finally disappear until about 2040 B.C. We are here ignoring this period of overlap, and rounding off the dates as above. (*CAH* I, 1, Ch. vi and chart on p. 996 of Volume I, 2.)

Under the Eleventh Dynasty, two powerful families began to reconstruct Egyptian power, from a base at Thebes. Ramses knew them well: the Intefs and the Mentuhoteps. For some 160 years this dynasty functioned, and it did leave monuments, notably the mortuary temple near Deir el-Bahri, the oldest such in Thebes. Cultural revival

led to a resumption of noteworthy reigns, especially that of Smekhere-Mentuhotep, who ruled 50 years and inspired Ramses.

This king conducted the first foreign enterprises in Egypt since the Sixth Dynasty, 500 years before. He pioneered a route through the Red Sea, and apparently fought back an obscure enemy in a sea-battle on the Nile. He even tried a pyramid, but could not afford stone. The sun-dried brick lasted poorly, though it remained in good condition when the Ramessid inspectors arrived a thousand years later.

There's evidence that Ramses noticed this energetic reign coming after a period of decline, just as the Ramessids succeeded the slack period of Akhnaton (see Chapter 4). the evidence is a colossus of Ramses as a votary of the god Montu, with his consort Rat-tawy. These two were worshipped at a temple near Thebes at Armant, or Hermonthis to the Greeks, also known as the Heliopolis (again, "sun city") of the south. (See the Montreal catalogue, no. 1. More detail: *Ramses le Grand,* no. 65.)

Of course the new sun-pharaoh wanted to be represented there. The link with the Eleventh Dynasty is that Montu had been virtually the patron saint of that dynasty, so much so that some of its kings named themselves after him.

Montu had a firm hold on the Karnak area, so that when Ramses later built heavily there, he used a plan which left Montu at the four corners, forming the palladium of the city and providing its divine protection.

Ramses put this statue before the temple of Montu, which has left traces of itself. His belt-buckle on the statue gives his throne-names, *Usimare-Setepenre,* and then calls him "Powerful like Montu." The statue was brought to Cairo in 1913, and it's a beauty, pink granite and about six feet high; it was in the Paris exhibition, and is in the travelling Exhibit.

Ramses calls Montu his "father" there, and the female counterpart, the sun-goddess Rat-tawy, his "mother." This cult assumed great importance for him, and as we'll see when he dressed for battle at Qadesh, it was as devotee of Montu. Another strong cult in the vicinity, that of the Buchis bull, sacred to Montu, lasted centuries more, and installation of a new one was the first official act in the reign of Cleopatra.

Another point not lost on Ramses was the idea of ruling Egypt from one end of it, though he was to choose the opposite end, for reasons appropriate to his time. The previous attempt to rule Egypt from Thebes back in the Eleventh Dynasty had succeeded. Whoever controlled the south of Egypt controlled it all, at that period. The great empires of aggressive expansion--Babylonians, Hittites, Mitanni, Assyrians--had not yet arisen to threaten the Delta or call attention to it. Rule from the south seemed feasible, since Nubia could be kept in check and the desert and sea might hold off all others. This thinking proved sound for another three hundred years, until the Hyksos came.

When in Egypt, one keeps looking around in amazement at how *old* the place is, and how long its history extended. Periods that seem to drop by the wayside as we rattle through their history--three or four centuries at a crack, sometimes--would more than guarantee a modern state. But things were more stable then, sad to say. To Ramses, regarding a predecessor from centuries before as a strong model seemed an entirely reasonable course.

The Twelfth Dynasty

We can detect some further influences on Ramses during the Middle Kingdom. The 200 years following 2000 B.C. saw major changes in the ancient world, for instance the settlement of the Greeks in their peninsula. The Minoans on Crete rose to the status of a major civilization, in close contact with Egypt. The Babylonian Empire established itself in power and its famous king and lawgiver, Hammurabi, ruled right at the end of these 200 years.

By this time, the great period of Sumerian history had ended, with probably few effects on Egypt. However, people remembered the Sumerians' mighty Ziggurats for many centuries, and Egyptians did too when they looked at the Step Pyramid of Zoser, visible from the Nile Valley near Memphis.

Under the Twelfth Dynasty, an important new dimension was added to Egyptian history, with eventual consequences for Ramses. This was the initiative taken about 1975 B.C. by Amenemhet I to establish footholds of conquered territory in Palestine and Syria. Just who his adversaries were is hard to document, since the population there were basically Canaanites, a term covering several tribal groups.

We do hear of a people called the "Sekmen," which is reminiscent of the "Shechem" of the Old Testament. In any case, this was the first real military expedition by Egyptians against Syria, and it set a theme followed for 800 years, down to Ramses and then beyond.

Other aspects of Amenemhet's reign also opened doors hard to close, such as renewed expeditions to Nubia, which was in fact for a time annexed.

Unfortunately, he was not to enjoy the rewards of this vigorous

career. One night, on his belly "like a snake in the desert," he heard some of his subjects searching for him. He opposed them, but "no man fights well at night" and he perished. As we learn from the vivid story of Sinuhe, who was there, that he had to flee the prospect of "civil disorder;" "I did not expect to live after him." (J.B. Pritchard, *Ancient Near Eastern Texts Relating to the Old Testament,* Princeton 1955, pp. 18-22.) Fortunately, the Middle Kingdom survived disruptions like these and continued the work of stabilizing Egypt.

No doubt that Ramses II was aware of Amenemhet I and his later successor, Amenemhet III. An extraordinary granite sphinx of either king, face muffled by the lion-mane, shows on its surface that Ramses found it. After sufficient exclamations of admiration he behaved according to form and usurped it. His own successor, Merneptah, subsequently did, too--followed by yet another admiring pharaoh, Psusennes I of the Twenty-first Dynasty. (Baines and Malek, p. 177.)

During this time the "middle class" was, in effect, the dominant one in the state, for the first and last time in Egyptian history of the pharaonic period. This constituted a type of feudalism. Control was maintained by the practice of requiring lands to revert to pharaoh upon the death of their holders. At Abydos, 800 tombs of these people have been found, some of them quite sumptuous. (There's one at the Oriental Institute in Chicago made of beautiful cedar.) The interesting link here is that Abydos was special to Seti I, father of Ramses II, and then to Ramses himself. We'll later see their work in constructing a major temple there.

The Middle Kingdom's Legacy

More facets of the early history of the Middle Kingdom descended to Ramses.

The Theban priesthood of the god Amun was notorious for its power in the land, especially during the Eleventh Dynasty, centered at Thebes for a century and a half. However, when the Twelfth Dynasty succeeded it, an important change was in the air. These new kings were also natives of Thebes, but they saw the dangers of ruling so far from the major populations. Accordingly, they moved the capital northward to Memphis. Its Egyptian name, It-tawy, which means "The Seizer of the Two Lands," is an apt description of its location and intended function. Ramses would not miss the significance of this move. He attempted to go it one better with Pi-Ramsese, his new city even further north.

One contemporary text shows a background of trouble when the Twelfth Dynasty took power about 1990 B.C., for a glorious period of rule lasting down to about 1785. The text says the king "restored what he found in ruins, and what one city had taken from its neighbor. ...He caused one town to know its boundary with another, and he established boundary stones as firm as the sky, for he knew their irrigated domains from what was in the writings." Here's the benefit of that concern with records and the croplands: potential order always lay behind disorder, since an appeal to records could settle disputes.

Religious Accommodations

Now, in restoring Egypt after the intermediate period, and in moving the capital, these kings had to make religious accommodations. Nobody dared face the priests of Amun directly. We can see from the behavior of Ramses how careful he had to be, making a point of beginning his reign there despite his intention of eroding Amun's power. By early in the Twelfth Dynasty, popular loyalty had shifted toward the alternative sun-god, Re (after whom Ramses was later named). If Egypt were to remain united, something had to be done to reflect this.

The answer was typically Near Eastern, and it's called "syncretism." It had its limitations, but versions of it are visible all over the East at every period. They simply melded two or more gods, so far as they could. Thus in Egypt a new god arose, called Amun-Re, who let people have both at once. Essentially they were walking on eggs with this, but Ramses proved exceptionally good at it.

More Legacies

Architecturally, the Middle Kingdom left very little. They tried the last pyramids, modest ones but with cunning doorways and trick passages to protect the body. We know Ramses was aware of these monuments, of course, because there are records that his officials regularly inspected pyramids.

Another facet of Egyptian history probably began now--relations with the Aegean peoples, especially the Cretans and the Mycenaeans. Their pottery begins to appear in the tombs, and Egyptian trade goods are found up north. We don't often think of Ramses in this regard, because he lived just before the time of the Trojan War, when the Cretan civilization had collapsed and the Mycenaean was about to. There's more than generally known to show that Egypt retained its contacts, but Greeks didn't interest Ramses as much as Near Easterners did, so his wall-decorations don't tell us much.

The Middle Kingdom saw the legendary conquests of Sesostris III mentioned above, which Ramses so admired that he used a nickname based on that king's throne-name. His motto, "The true son fights as his father did," probably stayed before the sweating face of Ramses on his many campaigns.

Another inspiration came from the agricultural work of Amenemhet III, who built a retention wall 27 miles long at Lake Moeris and thus doubled the volume of Nile water available to Egypt. There were 27,000 acres at the lake alone. Amenemhet's building effort still impressed travellers in the first century after Christ, 18 centuries later; the Greek geographer Strabo saw a building so big he thought it was the ancient labyrinth. When Ramses usurped the statue mentioned above, we have a graphic illustration that he took pride in this ingenious predecessor's deeds. (Baines & Malek, p. 177.)

Much else remained from the Middle Kingdom for Ramses to think about, including some of the best Egyptian literature ever, and prophecies that he thought he could fulfill--interesting for the pharaoh of the Exodus.

New Directions

The Second Intermediate Period lasted from about 1780 to about 1567 B.C., covering the Thirteenth to the Seventeenth Dynasties. Did Ramses look with intense interest into this period of obscurity, when sometimes several kings ruled at once? No. He firmly rejected one principle which arose then, that the pharaohs could be elected, ruling through their viziers. He rested his own dynasty's case firmly on divine birth, and probably thought these kings had weakened Egypt. There was on one occasion even a Nubian ruling Egypt. Some of these kings actually bore Semitic names, and might show the beginnings of an infiltration that bulked large in Egyptian history. That was the occupation of Egypt by the dreaded Hyksos.

The Stele of the Year 400

A mysterious document from the reign of Ramses II vaults backward in time four centuries from his own day to that of the Hyksos. It shows the vividness this epoch left in the minds of Egyptians. The document, a monolithic red granite slab, was found in 1863 A.D., then lost, and rediscovered at Tanis in 1931. It's in the Cairo Museum, and went to Paris for the Exhibition in 1976. (See *Ramses le Grand,* pp. 32-38.)

Scholars know this thing as the "Stele of the Year 400." It shows Ramses and an official in standard poses, under the winged disk of the sun (now almost completely effaced). The god Seth appears promnently, with beard and tiara, and the stele contains a prayer to him. Ramses apparently means him when he speaks here of "the father of his own

60

fathers." The "fathers" are selected preceding kings of Egypt. A long recitation of the titles of Ramses occupies part of the stone.

One interesting remark brings up, in a list of officials, the name "Paramesses," apparently the same as Paramessou, the vizier whose statue was discovered at Karnak in 1913. He was recognized as the future Ramses I, founder of the Nineteenth Dynasty and grandfather of Ramses II. Two others mentioned on the stone may in fact be Seti I, father of Ramses, and Tuya, his mother, here identified as "a chanteuse of Re."

As a further point of interest, the stele refers to the date as in the "fourth month of summer, day four, in the year 400." This unique citation must refer to an event about 1700 B.C., connected somehow with the corner of the Delta where Ramses wants his new capital to be, and linked in a manner with the god Seth because of the god's prominence on the stele.

Through the controversies this stone has caused, we may see a remarkable commemoration. Ramses reaches back 400 years, to the time when the Hyksos occupied this part of the Delta and used Avaris as a capital from which to assume control of the remainder of Egypt. The Egyptian god Seth, creepy and foreign, may be receiving a new incarnation through them, established in the Delta with new temples (Ramses later built one to him there too).

Since Ramses also wishes to rule Egypt from this corner, it may be to his interest to demonstrate that it had been done before, though a related danger was the poor image the Hyksos had left.

Another theme in the stele lurks in these commemorations of his family. Since the early Eighteenth Dynasty, it had been possible for a pharaoh from outside the direct line to argue that he had divine birth

because his mother had been visited by a god. Even Hatshepsut tried this, and at Luxor the "Birth Room" chapel commemorated the idea. Ramses' mother, "singer of Re," might have claimed that she had conceived by that god, and her son duly bore Re's name as part of his own. The idea of a new golden age under a divine family should have awed Egyptians into accepting the dynasty of the Ramissids.

We have another possible reflection of all this in the "epoch of Menophres," a king whom Egyptians honored for another twelve centuries after Ramses, right down into Roman times. The name comes to us through Theon of Alexandria, a Greek from Asia Minor who moved to Egypt in the first century B.C. One view sees him trying here to write "Menpehtyre"--a coronation name of Ramses I. Perhaps this all reflects successful establishment of the notion that something new and permanent had occurred 400 years before Ramses, and then received fresh impetus through him and his family.

The Hyksos
(c. 1720-1567 B.C.)

Ramses had a mysterious connection with the Hyksos as did all of Egypt. Who were the Hyksos?

Until recently, people followed the version given by Manetho, an Egyptian historian of the third century B.C. who exists now only in fragments. Manetho wasn't entirely sure who they were, because he called them in various places Arabs, Phoenicians, or Judaeans. This was long before Jews arrived in Palestine, so he probably meant Canaanites when he said Judaeans, retrojecting from his own day.

Manetho laid another trap for his readers when he came to the name

THE ISRAELITES IN BONDAGE

by which Egyptians knew these people. Their term was, in hieroglyphics, *Hyku Shose* (Hq3 h3swt), which means "Rulers of Foreign Lands." He misread that as *Hyk-sos,* which would mean "Shepherd Kings." Manetho, in fact, was in error. Attempts to explain it all have postulated Syrian princes, Biblical patriarchs, tribal leaders from India, Hittites, and Mitanni, to name a few. It *is* obvious from their names that they were Semitic, names like Salatis, Khyan, Apophis. Maybe they were the edge of one of the great movements of peoples which occurred after 2000 B.C.

The sources aren't sure how they took power; Manetho says without a blow, but later implies a reign of terror. Josephus, the Jewish historian of the first century, says perhaps the Hyksos used Hebrews in Egypt as allies, and maybe brought them there.

The record shows no real break in culture or in burial customs, as we might expect with invaders. They do seem to have come from the Near East, because they used chariots and bronze weapons. Some of their scarabs are found in Palestine, and in Bagdad was found a cartouche of one king. These do not demonstrate their origins, since they are portable objects. However, they do show that relations continued.

The relevance of all this comes from our noticing that the Hyksos made their capital not Memphis, or Thebes, but that small city in the Delta called Avaris (later terms in the vicinity are Tanis, el Qantir, and Tell el-Dab'a). That area was the home of Ramses and his family.

For over 150 years, from about 1720 B.C. till 1560, these apparent foreigners ruled the region, and then all of Egypt, and they did it from up in the Delta. Ramses tried to do the same, building his new "turquoise city" (Pi-Ramsese) right next to Avaris. But there's more to it than that.

The Hyksos, whoever they were, wanted desperately to be legitimate sovereigns of Egypt. They took throne-names fully Egyptian in form, usually ending with the name of the god Re, and they managed to form what even Egyptians admitted were the Fifteenth and Sixteenth Dynasties.

Ramses would like to see that claim to acceptance stand, and his "Stele of the Year 400" seems to legitimize their stay in Egypt. He must have been aware that some would not have agreed, since the Hyksos were cordially hated. We have a text by Queen Hatshepsut, a century after they left and about 150 years before Ramses. She says, "I have raised up what had gone to pieces...since the Asiatics were in... Avaris."

We even have a schoolboy's copy-text from toward the end of Hyksos rule, copying a stele by one of the Egyptians who opposed them by creeping in between the Nubians to the south and the Hyksos to the north. It says, "One prince is in Avaris, another in Ethiopia, and here I sit associated with an Asiatic and a Nubian. Every man has his slice of Egypt, dividing up the land with me. But I'll go after the Hyksos king and will grapple with him to cut open his belly."

But were Hyksos foreign invaders? There's an alternative view. Professor Manfred Bietak, Director of the Austrian Archaeological Institute in Cairo, has long been excavating at Avaris (now called Tell el-Dab'a), the old Hyksos capital. His people have been finding not the camps of warriors, but what looks like a trading empire.

He finds not a sudden appearance of invaders about 1700, but instead a gradual building up since 2000 of a local outpost. It was probably started by pharaohs of the Twelfth Dynasty to guard the Delta. But it was abandoned and resettled by people importing oil and

wine, using jars made in Palestine and Lebanon. This was maritime trade, and it continued unbroken for centuries.

Why do people later resent the Hyksos so much? The reason explains the interest Ramses took in the Hyksos. The deeper emotions can be roused by a threat to established religion ("invading heathens," Crusades, Wars of the Reformation, "Godless atheists" as your enemy).

Well, what of Semites? If they had gradually infiltrated from Syria, they probably brought their own god with them. This god was Ba'al. Now, in the entire Egyptian pantheon, only one god fits the description of Ba'al, and that's Seth, beloved of Ramses, and the god of the Avaris region. What seems to have happened is that they fused him with Ba'al, and were content. In that text previously mentioned, Queen Hatshepsut sourly comments, "They ruled without Re, and Re did not act by divine command during their time." The Khamose stela remarks, "Now King Apophis made Sutekh (Seth) his lord, serving no other god, who was in the whole land, save Sutekh." (See also Breasted, p. 176.)

The Avaris excavations turn up now a seal in a public building showing Ba'al Zaphon, protecting a ship. To bring home the point, Ramses was to name one of his daughters Bint-Anath, Anath being the great Syrian goddess. He also laid out a sacred grounds for the Syrian goddess Astarte at Avaris, and built a temple to Seth.

He named a son of his SETHirkhopshef to accompany another son named AMUNhirkhopshef. He also promoted a childhood friend of his who was probably a Syrian though he has a mixed name-- Ashahebsed, who became royal cup-bearer and then helped construct Abu Simbel, where you can still see his work. Ramses wanted to

legitimize the Hyksos period in order to win popular acceptance for his new capital on the same site.

The Seventeenth Dynasty
(c. 1650-1567 B.C.)

The Hyksos ruled all of Egypt before they were finished. But about 1650 the Seventeenth Dynasty arose in Thebes to begin the work of expulsion. Interestingly, the Turin Canon (not an implement of war, but an ancient king-list now in Turin, Italy) lists the first ten kings of this dynasty in a separate group from the last six, who carried out the military exploits associated with expelling the Hyksos. In typical Egyptian fashion, this was expressed as a conflict of gods--Amun in Thebes opposing Seth in Avaris.

The newer evidence suggests that might not be far from the truth. In other words, what rankled was not domination by foreign "shepard-kings" but the dominance of a rival cult. Amun was on the way to becoming the national god, but the Hyksos stood in the way. Centuries later, when Ramses wanted to re-establish the god Seth, he had to deny this nationalistic crusade against Seth, and he had to Keep Amun "in his place." That's why his "Stele of the Year 400" specifically commemorates the introduction of the cult of Seth to that part of the Delta. Ramses wanted this to appear as a major event in Egyptian history. His attempt failed, although he was careful to build both a temple to Amun west of Avaris and one to Seth south of it. For good measure, he also in the east laid out a sacred ground for the Syrian goddess Astarte.

Expulsion of the Hyksos

We have reflections of Egyptian attitudes in the texts mentioned before from Josephus (*Apion* 1.14) and Hatshepsut (*JEA* 32, 1946, pp. 43-56). We also have traces of the expulsion, some of it amusing and some not. During the reign of Merneptah, the sun and successor of Ramses II, a story was written down referring to this period, by then some 300 years before. It says that the Seventeenth Dynasty ruler Sekenenre III received from the Hyksos king, Apophis, a complaint that the noise of the hippos in the Nile near Thebes prevented him from sleeping, down in Avaris. Hippos are noisy, but you wouldn't expect to hear them 500 miles away. Sekenenre replied that he'd look after the problem. (J.B. Pritchard, *Ancient Near Eastern Texts Relating to the Old Testament,* Princeton 1955, pp. 230ff.)

What the Hyksos king may have meant was that he knew of a conspiracy in Thebes to take over the government of Egypt, because we know that warfare ensued. We also have the body of Sekenenre, and we can tell at a glance he lost. He took at least five severe blows to the head and the evidence shows that his body was not recovered for several days, suggesting a real rout. He finally received a hasty mummification. (Photo: Steindorff & Seele, p. 28, fig. 7.)

That was not the end of the affair. We have the schoolboy copy of a stele erected by the successor of Sekenenre, a man named Khamose, threatening to eviscerate the Hyksos who had killed his father. We also have an eyewitness account of some events by a sailor, Ahmose the son of Eben (notice the Jewish name for his parent).

The sailor Ahmose commanded two ships in succession, the first named "The Wild Bull" and the second called "Appearing in

Memphis." Sea battles occurred near Avaris and land battles south of it. Ahmose says he received gold awards seven times, and one man and three women as slaves. One of his slaves has a Jewish name, one is Semitic, and another is apparently a Babylonian, named Ishtar-Ummi. That now reinforces the idea that the Hyksos were a mixed group of infiltrators rather than a homogeneous group of invaders.

After the Hyksos

Following the campaigns, the military arm of the Hyksos apparently retreated into Canaan, because the next campaign was there, at Sharuhen. Presumably, the population there was already related, as the modern theory assumes.

Some have said that when Ramses II later invaded Canaan, he could justify it by saying that the towns were honeycombed with Hyksos. He also followed here the lead of two kings of the Eighteenth Dynasty, Ahmose I and Amenhotep I. They had both charged off into that region to see if they couldn't reverse the tide, and give Egypt an empire of its own.

As sometimes happens, the Hyksos interval gave Egypt benefits to offset the evil of ruined towns. The country now had advanced weaponry--chariots, bronze and horses. It also had a new spirit, as conqueror of the terrible Hyksos. Regardless of the possibility that the Hyksos may not have been a difficult adversary, Egypt took considerable momentum from this event.

The results included establishment of the New Kingdom (1546-1085 B.C.), which saw Egypt's Golden Age, the greatest period it has ever

had. This began with the Eighteenth Dynasty, included the Nineteenth of Ramses, and ended with the descendants of Ramses in the Twentieth. Since our subject is Ramses, we'll look only at those many facets of the Eighteenth which directly affected him.

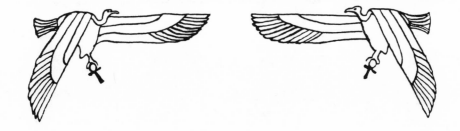

Chapter 3

The Golden Age

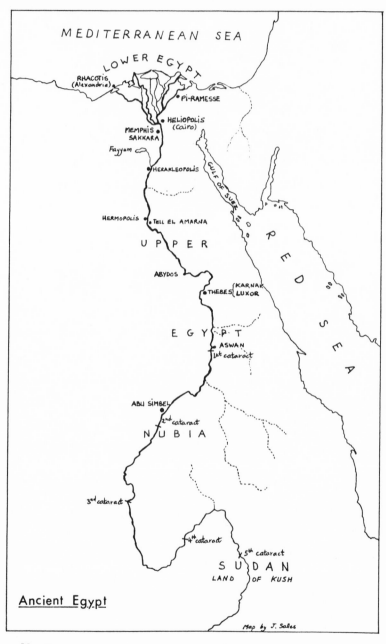

Ancient Egypt

MEDITERRANEAN SEA

LOWER EGYPT

RHACOTIS (Alexandria)

PI-RAMESSE

HELIOPOLIS (Cairo)

MEMPHIS
SAKKARA

Fayyum

HERAKLEOPOLIS

GULF OF SUEZ

HERMOPOLIS · TELL EL AMARNA

UPPER

ABYDOS

THEBES KARNAK
LUXOR

EGYPT

ASWAN
1st cataract

RED SEA

ABU SIMBEL
2nd cataract

NUBIA

3rd cataract

4th cataract

5th cataract

SUDAN
LAND OF KUSH

Map by J. Salles

No. 2

The New Kingdom
(1546-1085 B.C.)

The beginnings of the New Kingdom back in the Eighteenth Dynasty directly influenced the entire reign of Ramses II. He dreamed about Ahmose I and Amenhotep I, the founders of the New Kingdom.

The Eighteenth Dynasty
(c. 1546-1320 B.C.)

Ramses did not want people to miss the parallel between these kings and his own reign, which he regarded as the re-foundation of Egyptian glory. He also wanted to follow the example of Amenhotep, who became the first pharaoh to use a tomb in the Valley of the Kings west of Thebes, where his mummy has been found.

What Ramses recalled about the early days of the Eighteenth Dynasty were the expeditions against the peoples northeast of Egypt. Tuthmose I hacked his way clear to Syria and claimed to conquer it. The conquest lasted only till he was over the horizon, but he had left a stele on the Euphrates, on which he noted that the river "flows the wrong way."

Tuthmose also made it to the Third Cataract, where he left an inscription on the cliff. It says that Nubia is Egyptian territory once again, and Ramses had to spend much of his reign 200 years later to reinforce that claim.

Queen Hatshepsut

Tuthmose left behind a problem for Egypt. His daughter, Hatshepsut, was by his first wife; his eldest son, Tuthmose II, was by the second wife, and he began to rule when Tuthmose I died not long before 1500. (We have his body, too; he was the first of the pharaohs who were later re-buried in a common grave; more later.)

Now, these two children had been joined in a *philadelphic* marriage, in line with Egyptian royal custom. They had a daughter, and he had a son by a minor wife; so *those* two married also. Tuthmose II scratched out a short career for himself, though he was dominated by his sister-wife, Hatshepsut; he died about 1500 after the usual expedition to Nubia. That left Hatshepsut as "Royal Widow" but not as mother of the next pharaoh, her late husband's young son, Tuthmose III, by a different wife. On the reliefs his people carved, Hatshepsut is duly shown behind him.

Hatshepsut usurped the titles of the pharaoh, and the little ceremonial beard. The only title she declined was "Mighty Bull." She was now, in her own words, "*King* of Upper and Lower Egypt."

We have her description of herself. She's "exceedingly good to look upon, with form and spirit of a god...a beautiful maiden, fresh, serene of nature, altogether divine." Hatshepsut claimed to be visited by the gods, and began a vigorous reign. We have seen the text in which she claimed to rebuild after the Hyksos, and she did begin the first economic revival of Egypt since the Middle Kingdom.

She relied on an advisor called Senenmut, a man of humble origin who had gained high honors and perhaps was her lover too. There

wasn't a ready-made title for him either, so he became the "Great Nurse" of her daughter. That gave him access to the court. On one statue of him with the daughter, the little girl also wears the pharaonic beard.

Hatshepsut realized that her claim to fame would have to rest on deeds, and she didn't think she'd be all that good with a javelin, or in one of those chariots out in front of her troops. She saw a safer alternative: build mighty temples.

Ramses would never have admitted it, but he probably received part of his inspiration here, to become Egypt's greatest builder. He was obviously apprehensive about her reputation, because he systematically replaced her name on her buildings with his own. He wasn't altogether making a special case of her, because he occasionally did that to some of his male predecessors too. He relied in his reign on one device she had used just as Amenhotep III did: this was the idea that the god Amun had incarnated himself in the royal father at the moment of the royal mother's conception. (Kitchen p. 97) That made the child fully the offspring of the king, but also of the god. Ramses didn't call attention to her use of this myth, but he didn't mind people remembering that Amenhotep III had used it.

Hatshepsut created some beautiful things. Her description of one of her obelisks reminds us of the gold sheath those things wore. They're impressive enough without them, but imagine the sight with them. Hatshepsut says of these:

> I was seated in my palace, and I was thinking of the god
> who made me. My heart conceived the desire to erect in
> his honor two golden obelisks, whose points would

pierce the sky...I put them between the two great pylons of my father Tuthmose (I). You, who see these after many long years, you will speak of what I have done. You will say, "We do not know why these needles of gold were erected."

Hatshepsut anticipates the answer:

I lavished on them bushels of gold, as though I had been pouring out sacks of grain. Say, instead: "She did these things because she loved to do so."

The Obelisks

Most of the great obelisks come from Hatshepsut's reign or her family's. These are tall shafts of pure granite, often 90 feet high and in weight up to 1000 tons. A kind of instant pyramid, "piercing the sky," as she put it. They could get right up where the sun-god is and his delight would bounce in rays off the golden surface. A pharaoh did not have to wait up to 20 years, as he would if he tried to get a pyramid up.

We can imagine how attractive a big golden obelisk could appear to a conqueror. Beginning with the Assyrian Assurbanipal in the seventh century B.C., these things have been looted from Egypt. They now stand in New York, London, Paris, Rome, Istanbul (the one in the Hippodrome here shows the enduring quality of the granite, sharply contrasting with the weathered limestone base which is nearly two thousand years *newer*).

Some were gifts of the Egyptian government, like "Cleopatra's needles" in New York and London, brought there legally about 1880.

Their first trip had been to Alexandria about 23 B.C., just after Cleopatra's death but associated in some minds with her. Some never even left the quarry, like the famous one at Aswan which would have weighed 1170 tons but showed a crack and was abandoned, where we still see it.

These marvellous symbols of the Egyptians' reverence for the sun stood mainly in the great temples, especially Amun's at Karnak. Those which survive *in situ* still provide a shock of awe and recognition when one suddenly comes upon them pointing silently to heaven behind a high wall, or dominating a courtyard. Another motive for their construction is stated on the ones of Tuthmose III: "so that his name might endure forever."

Deir el-Bahri

Hatshepsut was remembered mainly for her magnificent mortuary temple at Thebes, called Deir el-Bahri now. It lies at the foot of the cliffs behind which hides the Valley of the Kings. It faces the spot Ramses II later chose for his own great mortuary temple, the Ramesseum. He realized that she already dominated this spot, of course, so he simply changed the ruler's name everywhere he found it on her temple.

Ramses may have derived an important inspiration here, for unlike most Egyptian temples, Deir el-Bahri is not free-standing, but carved deep into the cliff, just as he was to do with Abu Simbel.

Hatshepsut built on the grand scale. The major terrace rises some 160 feet above the base of the temple-complex. Some of the galleries

penetrate hundreds of feet into the cliff. The quality of carving is high, and lively. She prided herself on expeditions she had sent south into Africa in search of wealth and in hopes of reviving trade.

Especially fascinating to Egyptians was the "Land of Punt," by which they meant the modern Somali coast. In her ninth year she sent five large sailing ships there, and they discovered the "terraces of myrrh"--a most valuable product. They were quite taken with local dwellings built on piles in the myrrh-groves and reached by ladders. These appear on the walls of Deir el-Bahri, along with pictures of the personnel. The substantial Queen of Punt earned a measure of awe from Hatshepsut. (Photos of Punt: Steindorff & Seele, figs. 26 & 27. Also in J. Hawkes, *Pharaohs in Egypt,* New York 1965, p. 65.)

Tuthmose III

All this time Tuthmose III was growing up. He may have been married to Hatshepsut as a measure of legitimizing her, and he certainly was married to her daughter by Tuthmose II. Around 1482 B.C., Tuthmose III finally seized the throne from Hathsepsut.

Tuthmose obliterated Hatshepsut's name from what monuments he could, leaving the rest of the task to Ramses over a century later. She outsmarted them both by having her name carved in hidden places, where it has since been found.

Tuthmose III ruled more than thirty years in his own right after this (1482-1450 B.C.). He also counted the twenty years he'd ruled jointly with Hatshepsut, for a total of about 54. Here's one source for the conviction of Ramses that a long reign is necessary to get any real work done.

We know that Ramses found this reign fascinating. It's no accident that we discover their statues together, as in one line-up which features Tuthmose III, Ramses II, and Amenhotep II. These are red granite, from the seventh pylon at Karnak; Ramses has taken over two of them, originally for Tuthmose III. (C.F. Nims, *Thebes of the Pharaohs,* London and Toronto 1965, p. 67 with plate no. 30.)

A couple of points to raise about the view Ramses took of Tuthmose III, whose grinning mummy reflects his life of extraordinary accomplishment and satisfaction. If we required a precise model for the career of Ramses, we couldn't do much better. Both men attacked Syria and Canaan; both fought at Qadesh. On the way there, both fought in the area of Megiddo, from which we get the term Armageddon; its "capture was that of a thousand cities" in the excited prose of its conqueror. Tuthmose took it after a seven-month siege, and was pleased at the inhabitants' response: "They begged breath for their nostrils."

Both pharaohs took personal risks. Tuthmose nearly lost one battle at Qadesh because a mare wandered out into the line of battle-stallions. He fought personally, as any pharaoh did, and had to be saved by one hero from being trampled by an enemy elephant. Both dealt with the Babylonians. Both alternately threatened and exchanged gifts with the Hittites. Both left monuments in virtually every city of the realm.

Tuthmose, and Ramses in his turn, went for burial in the Valley of the Kings and both were later removed for reburial. The tomb of Tuthmose was a beauty, with a 65 feet shaft and 741 depictions of the gods. Ramses may have known how sumptuous it was. It even contained the complete Book of the Dead.

Finally, both lavished buildings on the Karnak complex, where both tell the stories of their campaigns. Tuthmose gives three lists of conquered towns, and proudly records tribute from Palestine, Assyria, Syria, and elsewhere. Tuthmose conquered areas even Ramses couldn't reach, such as parts of Media, Persia, Bactria, and Asia Minor. That was the high-water mark of Egyptian conquest ever, in the north.

Ramses received the credit, however, as we learn from a famous incident in A.D. 19. The Roman prince, Germanicus, brother of the Emperor Tiberius, visited Egypt and heard the deeds of Tuthmose read to him from the temple wall at Karnak. But when he asked who had accomplished these feats, the guide, who probably couldn't read hieroglyphics, or at least make out what the various throne-names meant, studied the wall a moment and then answered: "Ramses!"

The Golden Age

Tuthmose III is the pharaoh for whom a text- fragment reports a vision from the sky, a ball of fire with an odious smell emanating from it. Tuthmose and his soldiers watched it, and then rose and disappeared. Von Daniken attributes this reading to Alberto Tulli, formerly keeper of the Egyptian collection in the Vatican Museum. What it proves, I have no idea, if in fact it exists. (E. von Daniken, *Chariots of the Gods?*, Bantam paperback, 1971, p. 60.)

Tuthmose inaugurated the Golden Age of Egypt. Whatever we may think of empires, they tend to enrich the center. The ruling power sends agents out to the far regions of the empire and the money collected pours into the capital city.

Amenhotep II

Amenhotep II took his turn about 1450 B.C., ruled 25 years, and left a different type of model for Ramses to follow. His athletic prowess extended to all the traditional sports for a young pharaoh, especially archery. He bragged that no one else could even draw his bow--a theme borrowed by Homer for Odysseus--and that he could shoot through thick plates of copper, one arrow penetrating while another was already on the way. A classics professor in Toronto who has become expert on ancient bows has tested this claim and found that the ancient Egyptian recurved laminated bow--we still have some of them--could in fact be made that heavy.

An episode-stele found not long ago near the Sphinx reveals that Amenhotep excelled also at rowing, running, and hunting. He was a formidable warrior, and of course attempted a campaign against Syria. He boasted in his account of this that he not only conquered seven major princes, but brought them back to Egypt head down. From Palestine he hauled some 90,000 prisoners out of a multitude of towns and he earned tribute gathered hastily by the alarmed Babylonians and Hittites.

His tomb was broken into about the tenth century B.C., but was resealed after the rancid bodies of nine other pharaohs had been concealed there, including Tuthmose IV and Amenhotep III. In 1898, these pharaohs were rediscovered safely interred, and were taken to Cairo.

Tuthmose IV

Tuthmose IV left another type of precedent for Ramses to follow. He married a Mitannian princess--an Iranian. He had some minor campaigns to his credit, but is mainly noteworthy for his inscription between the forepaws of the Sphinx. It says that he nodded off one day near its head and dreamed that the whole enormous body lay unrevealed in the sand, 240 feet long. Tuthmose then began excavating. The job has been done several times since, in antiquity and in the last 200 years.

One graphic indication that Ramses was aware of Tuthmose IV is in the travelling Exhibit. On Elephantine Island, the emperor Trajan, who lived fourteen centuries after Ramses, built a monument and reused some columns he found there. One of them had a painted sandstone drum decorated with yellow hieroglyphs of Tuthmose IV. If we look carefully at it, and there are also the names of Ramses, engraved in intaglio in his favorite color, turquoise, as well as in red and yellow. (Montreal catalogue, no. 3.)

Ramses has been accused of usurping this drum, but he left the name and titles of Tuthmose intact and simply added his own message. When he discovered the drum, it was already more than a century old, so he respected it. It's a chance and dramatic trace of his constant activity to keep the past of Egypt alive.

The falcon above his head holds what they called the *shenu* ring. That represents the sun's circuit and when elongated it becomes the cartouche around the king's names, a lozenge-shaped circle. The whole ensemble here protects the pharaoh, who wears a headdress called the

khepresh, with the coiled uraeus cobra which served as another bodyguard. Ramses holds a bouquet of lotus flowers with the stems looped, and probably raises it in honor of Tuthmose, who is mentioned in the text. The bouquet suggests rebirth, just what Ramses wants to claim for his reign.

Just above Ramses' forehead are two of his royal cartouches. The first has his coronation name, *Usimare-Setepenre,* then the titles identifying him as king of South and North, and son of the Sun. Then the birth-name, *Ramessu-Meryamun,* "he who has life like the sun."

His belt-buckle has the coronation titles again. He has a linen robe, and the wide necklace called *wesekh,* of course made from gold. His mummy shows that Tuthmose IV died young, as is known from his records, as well.

Amenhotep III

Both Ramses and his father openly modelled themselves on Amenhotep III. Seti I wanted to seem the most valiant warrior since Tuthmose III and the greatest builder since Amenhotep III. When he called himself *Men-ma-re* ("of lasting right is Re"), he used one element *(Men)* from the titles of Tuthmose *(Men-kheper-re)* and another element *(ma)* from the titles of Amenhotep III (Neb-ma-re). (Kitchen, p. 20.)

He also used epithets favored by Amenhotep and not used since his reign: "Heir of Re" and "Image of Re." Also, the word for "rebirth" occurs right at the beginning of his reign in his account of his first

campaign. We'll see later that he pitched right into Karnak in an effort to pick up where Amenhotep III had left off. Ramses followed Amenhotep in other regards, too, by building rival temples far to the south.

Another respect in which both followed the Eighteenth Dynasty lead was through use of high-profile architects. The man who built the great works of Amenhotep III used that same name, with a nickname "Huy." This is the one who says, "I did not imitate what had been done before." He built marvellous things, including a temple at Luxor and a huge temple across the Nile for Amenhotep. All we have left of this second one is the two enormous guardian statues in front, now called *The Colossi of Memnon,* each originally about 70 feet high and weighing some 450 tons.

The Architecture

As demonstrated by his portrait-statue now in Cairo, the architect Amenhotep-Huy, son of Hapu, possessed the shrewdest old face most of us will ever see. (Steindorff & Seele, Fig. 18.) He knew how much the people admired him. Egyptians regarded architects with great awe. As with other Egyptians, he had a full career outside his "specialty": general, Chief Royal Scribe, and status among what the later Greeks knew as the Seven Sages, whose sayings were still quoted 1300 years later.

Ramses recalled not only the wise sayings, but the buildings. He saw the one we're no longer able to, in West Thebes the Colossi of Memnon. He saw the marvellous constructions in Luxor and Karnak.

Huy had attempted probably the world's first basilica-form building, at Luxor. It stood incomplete in Ramses' day, as it still does; he happily added his own pylon to it. (Steindorff & Seele, Fig. 41-42.)

The type is properly described as columnar, axially symmetrical, with a central clerestory. That is, to take for example the developed version at Karnak, the columns are of two different heights, a central row of twelve of them about 80 feet high, then flanking rows of shorter columns. That makes the central ones project far higher into the air than the others do, and gives the opportunity for windows along the sides of the higher central part.

That describes the classical basilica (that term comes from the Greek word for "king," and shows the building type's purpose among Greeks and Romans) it had. We need little introduction to this form of building, since we use it all the time for our larger halls and public buildings. Mediaeval feasting-halls are usually of that type. We use that form most often in our greater churches and in the cathedrals.

Huy and Amenhotep III realized the potential of the columnar building more completely than anyone had before, and when Huy says "I did not imitate" he may be announcing the discovery of this great architectural form. Ramses and his father saw its potential and seized upon it for their greatest work, the Hypostyle Hall at Karnak. That's just a part of one great complex, but all by itself it became a wonder of the ancient world.

Queen Tiy

Amenhotep III set other precedents that Ramses noted. One was the matter of wives. Most of the pharaohs preferred to marry princesses.

Amenhotep III selected instead the beautiful commoner, Tiy, and the monuments duly notice that she became not only queen but Great Queen, that is the reigning favorite. We have scarabs announcing their marriage, and we have evidence that she stepped into the role in traditional form, getting fully involved in the international scene. As with two of the queens of Ramses, the Great Queen was expected to keep up a lively correspondence with foreign queens and kings, and even to comment on policy.

Tiy probably did that, because her official scarabs (small, beetle-shaped seals identifying their owners) are found up north in Crete, in the ruins of Knossos. They have been argued to be of importance in dating the great destruction there, since on one reconstruction they're found both above and below the destruction levels which signal the end of Minoan civilization. That would mean that the eruption which did the damage occurred during her lifetime, about 1412 to 1375--the regnal years of Amenhotep III. However, the circumstances of the seals' finding do not allow firm deductions, since disturbance may have occurred.

Tiy is depicted on some statues of equal size with the pharaoh, showing he wanted to leave no doubt as to her status. Her parents had the unusual honor of burial in the Valley of the Kings, where their mummies were found intact. Their blond hair may provide some clue to their daughter's success, if it was distinctive. (Steindorff & Seele, figures 15-17.)

We know that Seti I and Ramses II thought Amenhotep would make a superb model. It's possible that Seti even knew him. Not only did the two pharaohs echo his throne-name, but they followed his lead

Northwind Picture Archives

**ARCHITECTURE FROM ANCIENT EGYPT
NOTICE SIZE OF HUMAN FIGURE**

in emphasizing the role of both Amun and Ptah, naming some of their sons after these gods the way he had. One superb relief of Seti as pharaoh and Ramses as prince shows them venerating the cartouches of their royal ancestors, and Amenhotep is prominent there. (Kitchen, p. 12, figure 4.)

The titles of Seti echoed those of Amenhotep. His decorative schemes did too, especially at Karnak, depicting battles or the barge of Amun. The *scale* of his and Ramses' buildings shows a direct attempt to recall his work and then to surpass it.

A mysterious, wasting disease beset Amenhotep III late in life. We can pick it up on the depictions of him, which are remarkably candid and unflattering. (Steindorff & Seele, Fig. 20.) We also have his mummy, terribly emaciated. His body in the paintings or engravings looks flabby, lethargic. He may have passed this on to his son.

The empire established by Tuthmose III began to decline markedly late in the reign of Amenhotep III, and worse was to come.

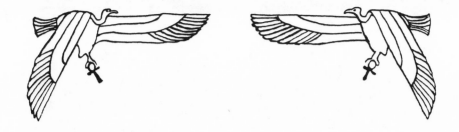

Chapter 4

Akhnaton's Revolution

AN EGYPTIAN SCENE

Akhnaton's Revolution
(1379-1362 B.C.)

Amenhotep IV succeeded at his father's death in 1379; he may have been associated on the throne for several years prior. The transformation of his name from Amenhotep to Akhnaton accompanied the religious changes he introduced.

Akhnaton has always received a "bad press," as it were. The times required a vigorous pharaoh on the lines of Tuthmose III. Akhnaton was unable to earn the respect of his contemporaries. This is how he has been portrayed. (Steindorff & Seele, Figures 21a, 73, 75, 83.) At best, he was not an imposing figure, with a soft body and round little "beer-belly." Modern descriptions employ such terms as "hideous," "grotesque," or "misshapen." Akhnaton, through choice, led an austere life. He had unlimited politcal power, but it did not interest him except for ensuring his religious autonomy.

Akhnaton decided to start a new variant of the Egyptian religion, but hardly found a receptive audience. Egyptians moved excruciatingly slowly in matters sacred, and we can imagine how people like Ramses later reacted. True that Ramses tried to push the cult of Seth, but not in opposition to anybody else.

The Religious Reform

He became a religious mystic, and became convinced that the true god was not the sun but the part of it known as the *Aton*. This is the aspect of it that stays in the eye after you glance directly into the sun.

91

He reasoned that this central disk must be the essence of the sun--
where the nutrients came from, so to speak. He could see the swirling
light in there, and thought it might be speaking to him.

Here is his own summary, given in a beautiful "Hymn of Praise" he
probably wrote. It was found on the tomb walls of Ay, the pharaoh
who succeeded Tutankhamun. He says:

> You appear beautifully on the horizon of the heavens,
> O living Aton, who were the first to live. You rise
> on the eastern horizon and fill every land with your
> beauty. You are lovely, great, dazzling, and exalted
> over every land. Your rays embrace the lands to the
> outermost limits of all you have created...
>
> The two lands are in festival, people awake and
> stand on their feet, for you have raised them up.
> They wash their limbs and put on clothing. Their
> arms are lifted in praise, when you rise. The whole
> earth goes about its tasks, the beasts rest in the
> meadow, trees and plants grow green, birds flutter
> from their nests and their wings praise you. Every
> wild creature springs forward on its feet...Ships
> ply the Nile and every road opens when you appear.

And so on: he covers fish, childbirth, chicks emerging from eggs,
cattle, foreigners (in Kush and Syria), the underworld. He says:

> You set everyone in his own place and you care for
> his needs. Mankind's tongues and ears are divided
> by language...you have distinguished the nations.
> You're the one who created the Nile in the underworld.
>
> When you rise as the living Aton, gleaming and

dazzling, far away and yet near, you make millions
of forms from yourself alone--cities, villages, fields,
roads, the river. Everyone beholds you before him,
for you are the orb of the day above the earth.

People wonder if this is now monotheism, and it's a good question.
He does have the Aton show itself forth in everything. But the other
side is that he didn't erase the existing cults. He tried to downplay
Amun, and he altered the old form of Aton's name to root out Horus.
But he had to admit the importance of Re, and makes the Aton to be
the manifestation of Re as an incarnation. "Re lives, ruler of the
horizon rejoicing in the horizon in his name of father Re, who has
returned as Aton."

The Theban priests of Amun especially disliked a new rule against
making statues of the god as a person; all one could show was the disk,
the sun's orb. To drive home the point that change was here, at this
point Amenhotep IV altered his name to Akhnaton. Instead of
retaining a name which meant "Amun is satisfied" (he definitely was
not), he became "He who is beneficial to Aton." He even reworked the
reference to Amun out of his father's name on the monuments.

All this meant he had better found a new capital, just as Ramses later
did. His new city was called Akhetaton, "The Horizon of Aton." That
city still exists, called Amarna by the local Bedouins. Akhnaton
ordered a sumptuous city built. The excavators have found temples,
palaces, and other such necessities remaining from the city.

At first, Akhnaton tolerated some of the other gods, but by his sixth
regnal year it was law that Aton reigned supreme. This is vividly
reflected in, for instance, Tomb no. 82 at Thebes, where inscriptions

from the reign of Tuthmose III were partly erased in the Amarna period to remove references to Amun.

Consequences

In the meantime, the empire started to slip. In the archives of his new city we have the so-called "Amarna letters" which poured in now from officials in Palestine and Syria. They're pitiful to read, because they call for help even as the enemy approaches. The empire eroded at speed. It wasn't until the reign of Ramses that this erosion was effectively reversed.

Akhnaton would not inspire many soldiers. He appears to have been flabby, even effeminate, no recommendation for a fighting man. He might have had that lethargy his father did toward the end. The new style of art in the palace favored realism, which was merciless for him. He's portrayed as slack and pasty.

The Court

His Great Queen, Nofretete (Nefertiti), may have been a Mitannian princess (from up beyond the Euphrates, where the pharaohs acquired princesses every couple of years). Other surmises see her a product of the royal line.

She has tormented people since antiquity, mainly because the sculptor of the the famous bust in Berlin became so enraptured that he forgot to finish her left eye. (Photo: Steindorff & Seele, Fig. 74.)

Anyone who ever wondered about the profile view now knows. Quite a story may lie behind that statue, as it does behind her life. She seems to have fallen out of favor with Akhnaton and had to move across town into another palace for the last years of his reign.

Amarna

Akhnaton seems to have been an average man. But he had no military interests and only the minimal interest in politics necessary to carry on his reign. His main absorption had been with his cult, even before his father died.

For the last ten or twelve years that Amenhotep III reigned, Akhnaton may have participated increasingly in government, though the evidence does not support the conjecture that he served as formal co-regent. He took advantage of that period to begin his reforms.

He began work on Amarna in the fourth year of this period, with no objection from his father. This grew into an entire district, with both banks of the Nile and a large level tract of land. It included several towns or villages, and a whole network of fields and canals. All of this belonged to the god Aton, with a resident priesthood. Akhnaton decided to move there, in his sixth regnal year.

Akhnaton prepared for the move by ordering construction of a fabulous building. If it had been completed according to the master plan, it would have ranked as the largest non-religious building in the ancient world!

It had an enormous reserved area, with a whole industrial and residential quarter in its complex, and long wings of brick which now lie under the fields but will one day be excavated. The state quarters

were stone, with a columnar entranceway and an unprecedented overpass into the town, like Nero on his flyover from the Palatine to his Golden House, safe from the groundlings.

It had the usual "window of appearance" where the king and queen could look down at the multitude and hand out the golden rings or collars that people always hoped to earn.

Life in the Palace

Much of the building was completed, and much of it survives. We know a great deal aboaut the intimate details of life there, because the court itself delighted in painting these, and in producing sculpture.

One of the loveliest child portraits ever produced anywhere is one painting, which comes from the palace and can now be seen in the Ashmolean at Oxford. (Photo: Steindorff & Seele, Fig. 78; Davies and Gardiner, *Ancient Egyptian Paintings,* Plate LXXIV.) It shows two of the little daughters of Akhnaton, probably by his "Great Queen," Nofretete. They have the slightly misshapen bodies that the whole family came to be known for, and the elongated heads.

However, the moments of tenderness here portrayed are something new in Egyptian art, which had usually kept the pharaoh and his family out of sight in that regard. They were gods, after all, and should not be seen off guard. But the revolution changed things, and this new style at Akhetaton (Amarna) never blinked.

In sculpture, the same unflinching attitude. We know the chief sculptor of the place, Thutmose, and have a number of his finished

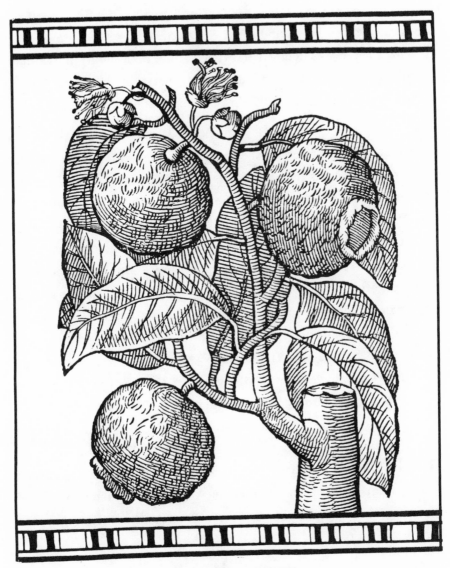

POMEGRANITE

products, as well as a few preparatory molds. (For the so-called "portrait heads." see Steindorff & Seele p. 213.)

This all gives us a detailed and vivid picture of the many individuals who lived here for an intense twenty years or so, from before Akhnaton's accession right through his estimated seventeen-year reign.

We have information on the town from tomb-paintings, and from the excavations, but the point for us is how did this influence Ramses? He undoubtedly passed through here on his many trips up and down the river, and he may have ordered some of it destroyed, but for the most part it was allowed to set neglected until the desert covered it. Nobody moved the state archives, which were probably considered best forgotten. Palace furnishings were abominations, so they stayed. Akhnaton just drifted into history and Ramses probably thought it best to leave the whole period in obscurity. So did the Egyptian court annalists, who treated Akhnaton's reign as if it had never occurred.

Ramses may have learned a thing or two, though. The new city had been designed according to a uniform plan, and all the administrative houses followed the same pattern. Central planning was an old idea for the Egyptian state, but not usually for its towns. When Ramses came to build his own new city, Pi-Ramsese, he had details already worked out for him by the town planners of Amarna. Even the very idea of founding a new Ramessid city may have arisen when Ramses gazed upon Amarna.

Nefertiti

Whatever killed Akhnaton might have taken a long time to do it, as with his father. The unblinking realism of the court artists produced those steady, clear, almost cruel portraits of him and the family. If Nefertiti was not Mitannian but in fact related closely to him, then she probably also displayed the family's physical characteristics, which we may detect in some portraits of her.

What went wrong in her relations with Akhnaton we don't know, but she did move to the north of the city, where a new palace went up for her. It has been excavated, and some of the objects found there indicate that young Tutankhaton (Tutankhamun) now lived there too. He was about five when she moved.

When she was gone, Akhnaton looked around for a replacement wife and his choice may have fallen upon Meritaton. She seemed to have the qualifications for queenship, since she was of royal blood. The only trouble is that she was his own daughter. As we'll see with Ramses II, who married at least two of his own, this was not an impediment among Egyptian royalty.

Smenkhkare

Whatever his intentions regarding Meritaton, she soon turns up married to a man called Smenkhkare, who may have moved into the palace as the co-regent. He soon drops out of the records at the palace, but one notice puts him at Thebes and mentions that he's in his own "year 3." So, he did rule.

If he's down in Thebes, was he sent there to mollify the clergy of Amun? That would have been a tricky assignment, and it's not surprising that one reconstruction has him and perhaps Meritaton killed down there. (Steindorff & Seele, p. 221.)

Ankhesenpaton

The third daughter of Nofretete, Ankh-es-en-paton, was now about 13. Akhnaton married her, and eventually she had a daughter, whom he named Little Ankh-es-en-paton. However, that did not give him an heir. When he died about 1362, Tutankhaton became the pharaoh, as Smenkhkare was apparently dead (if he ruled, it was only for a year). Ankh-es-en-paton then became King Tut's wife.

Dows this mean he wed his own sister? That depends on whose son Tutakhaton was, which is uncertain. Some think he was a younger brother of Smenkhkare, others that he was a brother of Akhnaton. At any rate, it seems that he descended from Amenhotep III, who may have been his grandfather. That was enough to guarantee his legitimacy as the new pharaoh.

Tutankhamun

(1362-1353 B.C.)

At this time, Syria was in revolt, allied with a group called the Habiru, from which we probably get the word *Hebrew*, though they're not the same group. There's a hated heresy as the religion of the land,

and the new royal couple even honor Aton by their own names. Tutankhaton means "Beautiful in life is Aton" and Ankhesenpaton means "She lives for Aton." The Vizier, an old man named Ay, convinced the reigning couple to change their names to the equivalent formula honoring *Amun*. They became Tutankhamun and Ankhesenamun. An astute move, but we can find objects in his tomb which were so exquisite nobody had the heart to change the artwork. The orb of the Aton still beams down from the superb little throne found in his tomb.

If the body of Tutankhamun had not been found in a resealed tomb, nobody now except professionals would have heard of him. Tutankhamun was "out of his league," and it was Ay who ran the government. Young Tut and his wife spent most of their time hunting ducks in the marshes, where--to judge from the paintings--she had to tell him which way to point. (For instance, Steindorff & Seele, Fig. 94, from Cairo.) With the bowstring behind his head, he wasn't going to get off a shot anyway. But a palace sharpshooter probably synchronized with him.

The court moved out of Amarna and back to Thebes. Akhnaton had once said his new religion would last "until the swan grows black and the raven white, until mountains walk and rivers flow uphill." Well, as with some of the Indian treaties, those conditions must have come to pass, because the ruins at Amarna and elsewhere show systematic effacing of the cult.

Akhnaton was striken from the pharaonic lists and his effigy destroyed wherever found. References to him call him the "criminal of Akhetaton" and the city was abandoned forever.

101

The Deeds of Tutankhamun

Tutankhamun responded to the public mood. Out of the palace emerged denounciations of the Aton heresy:

> I made falsehood to be an abomination in the land,
> as in former times...I suppressed evil and re-established
> justice.

He scurries to shelter under the wing of Amon-Re. Safely there, he announces that

> from Elephantine to the Delta marshes, shrines were
> overgrown with thorns...roads ran right through the
> temples. The gods had turned their backs on the land...
> for their hearts were angry in their bodies.

A fever of renewal filled Egypt. Statues of gold, restored monuments, temple-estates with rich annual incomes, new ships for the religious processions on the Nile, hordes of slaves set to work.

Things began to recover. One painting in Tut's tomb shows Nubians bringing gifts in tribute. (Steindorff & Seele, Fig. 24. See also p. 226 on the tomb of Amenhotep-Huy, viceroy of Nubia.) Another, on the lid of a chest, shows the boy "steamrolling" Syrians, though there's no proof he ever did. He probably laid an ambush for some camel-drivers at the edge of the Delta, and won his military spurs that way.

If the claimed tribute from Nubia is real, it shows firm control by Egypt: they bring horses, chariots, gold and silver, cattle from the Sudan, even a giraffe. Egypt was on the way back.

Tut ruled only nine years or so, and died about age 18. We won't go into his tomb, where world-famed objects were found. We note only the heart-rending little final tribute on his chest of some withered

LIFE IN ANCIENT EGYPT

These men are treading grapes in a stone vat.

flowers, perhaps from his wife.

It's interesting that the usual sumptuous display of objects for a pharaoh was probably not yet ready, when he died, so the minions of the crown stuffed in a large number of things originally made for Smenkhkare!

If Tut could usurp things from his predecessors, his successors could do the same to him, and we have statues, for instance, of Tut which were usurped by Ay and Harmhab. (Steindorff & Seele, p. 227, fig. 85.) Ramses II may have acquired his taste for others' buildings and artifacts from what he knew of this process in Tut's day.

The Reign of Ay

When Tutankhamun died, around 1353, no crisis ensued, for he had a co-regent, the old former Vizier named Ay. In Egypt, whoever had the status to officiate at the all-important burial rites of the last pharaoh usually became the next one. This could set off rather a scramble, of course, at the death of a pharaoh.

In the present case, nobody else had sufficient authority to challenge Ay, so he became the next pharaoh despite lacking a close tie by blood to the family of Tut and his predecessors, unless the title he adopted, "the God's Father," rests on some such relationship. This did not exactly set a precedent, but it was useful when the Ramessids entered the same situation soon, also without demonstrable ties to the family.

Ankhesenamun

Ay had some trouble convincing the young widow of Tutankhamun that she should marry him now. She decided to make the best match she could, and found nobody left of the blood royal in Egypt. What then of the outside world?

The only other Great Power at the moment was the Hittite Empire. Assyria had not yet risen to its full height, and Babylon lay in decline. Mitanni had supplied royal princesses to Egypt, but never a king; it would not have sufficient stature, especially since it had recently suffered an embarrassing defeat by the Hittites. The Hittite monarch was the formidable Shuppiluliuma, one of the great names in ancient history, which is full of them.

Ankhesenamun, who is thought to be the queen named Da-ha-mu-un-zu in a letter discovered in the Hittite archives, didn't want Shuppiluliuma himself, but one of his sons. She says,

> My husband, Nib-khuru-ria (Tut's protocol name),
> has recently died. I have no sons. They say you have
> many. If you send me one, he shall become my husband.

The wary old Hittite asked for assurances, and she said, "It's a humiliation even to ask you, but I'm serious." Accordingly, he gave in and sent a son.

Unfortunately, the new pharaoh, Ay, decided she had overstepped her authority, and besides, he liked his job. The Hittite prince was ambushed and murdered; so perhaps was Tut's widow, who is never heard of again.

Ay made a bad blunder here, because Shuppiluliuma took revenge. He invaded Syria and threw out the Egyptians. When Ramses II came

to power more than half a century later, the dust had still not settled, and he had to fight Hittites partly as a consequence of this murder.

Reign of Harmhab
(1348-1320 B.C.)

When Ay died, around 1348, he left a tomb at Amarna which constitutes a real document of the events of his lifetime. Egyptians regarded him and Tutankhamun as former heretics, since he had been caught up in the Aton adventure. The monuments of both kings suffered the same fate as Akhnaton's did, being scrubbed of their names wherever possible. The next king declared, in fact, that he was a successor not of these three but of Amenhotep III! Rewriting history is not a modern invention. The Romans even had a technical term for it, *damnatio memoriae* ("wiping out the record").

Who became the next king? Here we have the last pharaoh before the family of Ramses, and you can see how dicey things were becoming. No question of finding a member of the royal line, now, so the kingmakers rummaged about the palace and discovered the ideal new man, a hardened general named *Harmhab*.

He started as a royal scribe the way so many did. A statue shows him as a scribe, with the full robe and the pencil case and palette. It's now in New York. At the time he never suspected that he would one day be pharaoh.

During the four years of his own reign, Ay had designated Harmhab "King's Deputy" and therefore presumptive heir, but that was no guarantee. Harmhab had sought to bolster his position by marrying a

woman named *Mut-nodj-met,* who just happened to be the sister of beauteous Nefertiti, wife of Akhnaton. It did nobody any good to be linked to the heretic, but if these two were descended from a branch of the Eighteenth Dynasty's royal family, that gave Harhab a shot at the best remaining title any new pharaoh could hope for.

It worked. For some 28 years, he ruled successfully. This was a crucial period for Egyptians, and they were glad to have a firm ruler. It helped that he was a military man. The army saw action again, perhaps even as far north as Ugarit and Carchemish, which had not faced an Egyptian army since the days of Tuthmose III over a century before. Serving happily in that army was the great-grandfather of Ramses II.

Seti

This man was called Seti, which means "the man of Seth"--that violent god of the eastern Delta. He had seen the end of the reign of Amenhotep III and he had never espoused the Aton heresy. He rose through the ranks to become a Commandant of Troops. That seems to be as high as he got, which left the very top posts such as Royal Envoy or Vizier out of reach.

Pramessu

Seti's son, Pramessu, entered the army as well. Pramessu means "Re has made him." When the reign of Harmhab began, about 1348, Pramessu was probably twenty years old.

We have a statue of him showing him as a scribe, too. (*Ramses le Grand*, p. 15.) This was set up near the tenth pylon of the Temple at Karnak, during the reign of Harmhab. It's made of polished gray granite. On its right arm are the words, "Harmhab, beloved of Amon;" on its right shoulder it reads, "Chosen of Re:" that's the title Ramses II later favored, and he wore it in exactly the same place.

Interesting to note is the three-part arrangement of his hair on the statue which was not the fashion in the Eighteenth Dynasty (when the statue was carved). It became the fashion among the Ramessid kings of the Nineteenth Dynasty.

Wild birds were hunted with boomerangs.

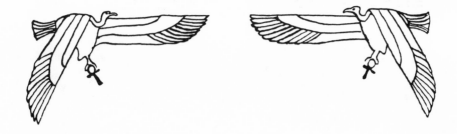

Chapter 5

The First Ramessids

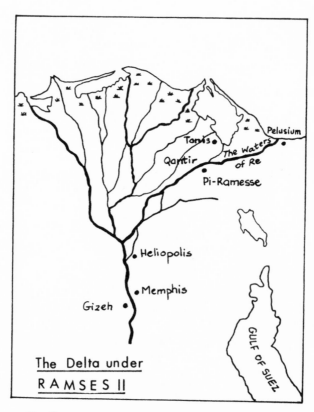

The Delta under
RAMSES II

No. 3

Transition to the Nineteenth Dynasty
(c. 1350-1320 B.C.)

Here in the reign of Harmhab (1353-1319 B.C.) lie the beginnings of the Nineteenth (or "Ramessid") Dynasty. The man called Pramessu was to become Ramses I, its founder. The reign of Harmhab constituted an excellent opportunity for those contemplating military careers. He had held supreme command of the entire army even before becoming pharaoh, and he knew how to rule the Two Lands as well as the possessions in Nubia and Syria. He also enjoyed great personal popularity, as Ramses II was later to do.

Harmhab utilized that to take power on the death of Ay, by marching on Thebes with the army and cowing all pretenders. He had already by that point won some overseas tributary lands, to judge from the paintings on his tomb at Memphis. These are some of the best of the realistic school ever known, and they show him presenting hostages to the pharaohs he served, Akhnaton, Tutankhamun, and Ay. Wen at last he seized his chance to rule, the pace of activity meant opportunities for eager young men like Seti and Pramessu.

We have some fine things left from the reign of Harmhab, right in the midst of later dedications by the Ramessids. For instance, his great pylon at Karnak. (Steindorff & Seele, p. 246, Fig. 96.) It carries a copy of his series of decrees designed, in his words, to "restore respect for law in Egypt...and destroy falsehood." The penalties for abuse of power usually caught one's full attention: loss of nose, followed by exile to a border town in the eastern Delta. Nobody knew which penalty was worse, coming after the high life of the capital.

We might wish that we still had the beautiful scenes which can even now be traced on the back of Harmhab's pylon. Unfortunately, the building program of Ramses I later led him right here, and the largest columnar hall in Egypt was slated to go in just behind it. That meant Ramses needed this space, for dirt fill and then to come up to the new roof-level. So, Ramses gave orders to erase all the splendid scenes of Harmhab.

Under Harmhab, things came alive, militarily and even commercially. The traders of Punt appear once again in the painted record, bringing their exotic wares up for sale, especially myrrh and the skins of rare animals.

The Nineteenth Dynasty
(1320-1200 B.C.)

By late in the reign of Harmhab, young Pramessu had risen high in the structure of offices in Egypt. He was already son of a Commandant of Troops, and he became one too. Then he rose to be Superintendent of Horse, that is head of the elite chariot corps. He was named "Commander of the Army of the Lord of the Two Lands" and "King's Charioteer." One jump away from that lay a post as Fortress Commander and Royal Envoy.

His appointment as Superintendent of the Mouths of the Nile led him back to his native district in the Delta. There he might face those from Canaan and the northwest who offered trouble; this category later included the dreaded Peoples of the Sea, whom Ramses II and then Ramses III had to meet. Pramessu became "Chief Justice," then Vizier, highest office in the land except pharaoh. These religious, political, and military posts imply single-minded determination.

Harmhab perceived his qualities and gave Pramessu perhaps the highest remaining sphere of honor: the right to set up twin statues of himself at Karnak beside the old sage, Amenhotep-Huy, the son of Hapu. This mighty lineup now brought him as high as one could go, with a title something like "Supreme Religious Official of All Egypt."

Harmhab reached his sixties and remained childless. Pramessu already had a son (Sethos I) and a grandson (Ramses II), so choosing him as a successor appeared safe: his family would not die out. In another way it bore risks, because these people demonstrated no connection to the family of the recent pharaohs. It would have been tricky had they shown close ties with Akhnaton, on the other hand, so a clean break of lineage seemed best, followed by a shrewd marriage.

By about 1320, Harmhab had designated Pramessu "Deputy of His Majesty in the South and the North." That let Pramessu represent Harmhab in any way events might dictate, civilly or religiously. He gained one last title, "Hereditary Prince in the Entire Land." Now the succession had been settled, always the delicate part when one tries to exercise a powerful monarchy and has run out of offspring.

Pramessu had reached a good age now, somewhere in his fifties, battle-hardened, experienced, and loaded with honors. When Harmhab died, his loyal Pramessu buried him, and to no one's surprise he did the burial honors, thus making himself the presumptive new pharaoh. He now founded the last great dynasty Egypt was to enjoy.

The new pharaoh had much to offer, especially in the matter of family. He was son of Seti, the Commandant of Troops who saw the

reigns of Akhnaton, Tutankhamun, Ay, and Harmhab. Ramses had a son and eventual successor, whom he also named Seti. This young man pursued a military career too, and he married within the military. His wife was named Tuya, and her parents are known. Her father was Raia, a Lieutenant of the Chariotry; he appears on a later relief with his wife, Ruia. (Kitchen p. 17, Fig. 7.)

The bridal couple, Seti and Tuya, had four children. Their first, a son, died young, as far as anyone can tell. Then they had a girl named Tjia. Years after the first, they had a daughter named Hent-mi-re, piously named for the sun god. In between the two daughters they had a second son, whom they named after his grandfather.

Ramses I

With a virtual dynasty being formed from him, Ramses I offered potential stability. He took power around 1320, using the high chronology. (W.C. Hayes in *CAH* I, 1, pp. 189-190.) He knew full well that Harmhab had chosen him for want of a son, and he knew he'd have to justify his position. Looking back through Egyptian history, he asked the court historian for parallels to his situation. The historian said that a nice parallel existed from the time that the Hyksos problem was met, 200 years before with Ahmose I.

Both Ramses I and Ahmose I were founders of a new dynasty. Both came at the end of a time of trouble--Hyksos then, Akhnaton now. Both began a period of military expansion, although the Eighteenth Dynasty did better in that regard than the Nineteenth was fated to do.

Both initiated a time of great achievement in architecture and the arts, fields regarded as of major importance in the ancient world. Both presided over the beginnings of a commercial empire, when Egyptians were not only proud, but prosperous.

The historian had to supply concrete reminders, and did. It may seem impossible to us that just by adopting some parts in the throne-name of a 200-year-old predecessor a pharaoh could make a statement, but we should remember that those names were well known to everybody who walked past any of the thousands of monuments standing in every district of Egypt. So if someone saw that the new pharaoh called himself *Men-pehty-Re* (which means "Re has lasting power"), one thought of Ahmose, *Neb-pehty-Re,* "Re is lord of power."

Ahmose had also called himself simply, "son of Re"--a plain title seldom if ever used in the next 200 years. So now Ramses became "son of Re" also. Ahmose used for his Horus-name "Great of Kingship"; Ramses took the name "Flourishing in Kingship," which looks almost the same in hieroglyphics. Ramses also used an archaic form honoring the god Amun, which would have been appropriate 200 years before.

The Architectural Program

Ramses I understood that a new dynasty had to win acceptance rapidly. One way in which to accomplish this was through architecture. The most powerful group in Egypt outside the royal family and the court itself remained the priesthood of Amun in Thebes, triumphant after Akhnaton's eclipse. In the future they were to prove fatal to the Ramessids, so we can see that Ramses was right to be wary of them.

He decided the safest course with them would be a massive monument, right in their front yard, at Karnak. One of his ambitions also was to remind people of the glorious days of Amenhotep III, and to suggest that he would make those days return.

He examined Karnak, and approved. Amenhotep III had begun there an enormous temple to Amun. The temple had in front a large courtyard, and Harmhab had just recently built his own pylon to stand before it, resplendent with polychrome decoration.

Ramses and his son, Seti, inspected the place. They decided on an enormous hall placed in the great courtyard of Amenhotep. The hall would contain gigantic columns, and would become the largest in the world. Unfortunately, the hall would not allow the beautiful scenes of Harmhab on the back of his pylon to show, so they would have to be erased. Respectful treatment of others' work was not to prove a Ramessid characteristic. Ramses I carved his own name right over Harmhab's wherever it occurred, to ensure that nobody failed to receive the message that power had now passed into new hands.

Ramses and Seti

This was the first act of the reign, as the new dynasty demonstrated its priorities. However, Ramses may already have been ill, for the work *he* might have done on the army fell to his son. Seti writes that "I rallied the army and gave it unity...I conquered for him the lands of the Fenkhu (Canaan, where the Jews later migrated)."

To the south, Ramses now endowed new temples and began to form the large work-force of captives that Ramses II later enjoyed. One of

Northwind Picture Archives

ARCHITECTURE FROM ANCIENT EGYPT

these temples, dedicated to Min-Amun at Buhen, stood as far south as the Second Cataract, well beyond Egypt's traditional boundaries.

The young prince, Seti, later modestly described his role in all this. If Ramses was the sun, then he was a star, reflecting the sun's light. "He was the gleaming Re, and I was with him like a star at his side." Ramses II later used a version of this doctrine of the reflected light in his Baboon Altar, which is in the travelling Exhibition of his artifacts.

Seti also managed to squeeze into the act when Ramses ordered a fine statue of himself near Thebes at the local temple of Montu (an important god to Ramses II). The statue carries the titles of both Ramses as "the image of Re" and of Seti as "the star of the land."

Ramses I had the glory and satisfaction of founding the Nineteenth Dynasty, but he did not get to enjoy it long. About a year and four months after his accession we find the mournful procession once more at Thebes, where his royal tomb had only just been started. Its corridor leads not to deep caverns far back in the rock as he had planned, but only to an unfinished antechamber, which was hastily plastered. The necessary scenes were not sculpted in low relief, since that takes time, but merely painted. A sarcophagus of red granite had to have its inscriptions painted on in yellow rather than incised.

Such the hasty last resting place of Ramses I. His son, Seti, officiated at the burial and thus became the next pharaoh, as both intended. His name is variously spelled in English as Seti, Sety, Sethi, or Sethos, and he becomes the first pharaoh named for the Delta-god Seth.

Seti I
(1318-1304 B.C.)

Before heading north again, Seti ordered his own tomb begun near his father's, and he inspected the continuing work over in the vast hall at Karnak. He changed the official name of the temple now to "Seti is effective." And so he was.

Around 1318 young Seti assumed full power. He was in his early thirties. Already he had experienced battle, and he possessed a ready-made family which included young Ramses II, probably about nine years old.

When Ramses I started the dynasty, he had chosen as a model the reign of Ahmose I, who expelled the Hyksos and began a new Egypt. Seti I adopted the idea, with a choice of models similarly inspired. He looked back into the early Eighteenth Dynasty and asked himself what was most to be admired there. It's instructive for us to see his choices.

The titles demonstrate his intent. His coronation epithet is *Men-ma-re* ("Re is enduring of Right"). As we survey the titles of Eighteenth-Dynasty kings, we see parts of that name in the reign of the great builder Amenhotep III *(Neb-MA-re)* and the great conqueror Tuthmose III *(MEN-kheper-re)*. Seti took one element from each, and let fly. He also employed titles not seen since Amenhotep III, like "Image of Re," and his Horus-name echoed that of Tuthmose III, "Mighty Bull Appearing in Thebes."

He also honored the god Ptah, of Memphis, in his titles, signalling a shift northward from Thebes, which he regarded as too far away to rule Egypt very well. He carried the epithet *Merenptah,* "Beloved of

Ptah"--and that's where Ramses II got this name for his thirteenth son, the one who in fact succeeded him.

The Ramessid Renaissance

Seti did not leave to the imagination what he intended for Egypt. Here's another title: "Bringer of Rebirth, Strong of Arm, Conquering the Enemy"--not only militarily capable, but an agent of renewal. *Rebirth* was a strong claim, not one that the Egyptians tended to use often. But things had grown so bad under Akhnaton that Seti saw no better way to pull people out of despondence than to trumpet a rebirth. A new era called "Repeating Births" was duly used by the scribes, often numbering his regnal years with reference to it, and the "era of Menophres" mentioned above probably preserved a classical echo of this.

It has been estimated that on the basis of precious metals and gems per capita, more wealth existed in Egypt and the Near East during the period of the Eighteenth and Nineteenth Dynasties and the preceding thousand years than ever before or since. We say per-capita to show how it's estimated, though of course most of it remained in the hands of the royalty and nobles.

Yet it was *there*--enormous amounts of gold and precious gems, with a considerable buying power in a semi-slave economy. A pharaoh's building program could include works on an enormous scale--not as great as in the pyramid age or the age of the Ziggurats in Mesopotamia, but still considerable.

Seti at War

If Seti wanted to restore the glories of Egyptian empire, he had a great, all-purpose excuse, because the empire was gone. Akhnaton saw to that. All Seti had to do was say, "Our imperial vassals have ceased to send their tribute" and he was ready to go. Treasury officials could reply, "Yes, in the time of our fathers, steady streams of bullion flowed from Canaan; who dares withhold it from *you*?"

Here's how Seti puts in, on one of the walls at Karnak, right at the beginning of his reign. "Year 1. The Renewal. King *Men-ma-re* (Seti), endowed with life. His majesty received the following message. 'The Shosu, our Beduin enemies, are planning a rebellion. Their chiefs defy us from their hilltops in Khurru (later Galilee). They are killing one another, and they ignore the laws of our Palace.'"

So, in they went. They were not reticent about this kind of thing. Read a little farther on the walls of Karnak: "His Majesty delighted at the news...he exults at the beginning of battle; his heart rejoices at the sight of blood. He loves to decapitate. He enjoys the moment of crushing (enemies)." He apparently even executed children: "He leaves no heirs." Seti thought he'd be feared if he couldn't be liked, and perhaps that was realistic for Egypt.

Seti's war-scenes at Karnak lie right in the Hypostyle Hall, and they stand in the fine old Egyptian tradition, showing the pharaoh always triumphant, with about forty arrows in play at a time, the horses excited, the enemy imploring mercy, the king shooting even as he rides, with the bowstring behind his neck. (e.g., Kitchen p. 21, Fig. 8.)

For decades, almost annual campaigns northward featured in his reign and that of Ramses II, usually through Gaza and into Palestine

(Canaan), then depending on his luck into Lebanon and even Syria, with a sea force landing near Beirut to come overland and help. Occasionally, the locals would assemble a large force and take a stand, as they did first at Beth Shan, the fortress at the eastern approach to the Plain of Esdraleon. (Photo: Steindorff & Seele, p. 249, Fig. 97.) There Seti won a small battle and left a stele we still have.

Seti did succeed at first, and soon developed a taste for more. Quite early in his boyhood, Ramses II began to accompany him. The little pharaoh-to-be even customarily "charged" in a small war-chariot. Adult soldiers were stationed carefully by to keep him in the rear guard, but Ramses would have some fun at little risk and would never know the difference. They might even have him discharge a few arrows, and report that he had "hit" somebody.

Seti and the Northeast

Seti marched from the Plain of Esdraleon north along the Jordan River and then to the occupation of Galilee and some of Phoenicia. There is a series of his stelae from Beth Shan. He records campaigns against "despicable Asiatics" and puts down a rebellion of the Apiru of Mt. Yarmutu. Again, "Apiru" isn't the Jews, though it may be where "Hebrew" and thus "Jew" ultimately originated. The connotation of the word had no necessary racial or tribal overtones, and was more akin to "brigand."

Seti penetrated into Syria, and the Anti-Lebanon Range. Soon he was near Damascus, and here he ran greater risks. He wanted this coastline, especially, because of the cedars--for the barges of Amun and for the great flagstaffs up in Thebes. Some 200 years later we have

a papyrus showing an agent of the priests of Amun in Thebes still sending out expeditions to bring back cedar. This is the Wen-Amon papyrus, and it shows how hard the locals would bargain, as Zakar Baal, a Syrian merchant, in effect equates the sale of cedar with an act of international politics, and says that if Egypt loses its power to compel in Lebanon and Syria, it will lose the cedar as well.

Seti had an even better reason to test the resolve of the Syrians as he moved north. He knew full well who was coming into Syria from the other side. The Hittites had been constructing an empire to control most of what is now Turkey. They had been up there for some seven centuries, and were approaching their zenith, if in fact they hadn't passed it fifty years earlier in the days of Shuppiluliuma.

The Hittites not only controlled part of Syria, but also regarded it as a permanent province of theirs, called *Amurru*. As Seti I states on his stelae, he hints that he has encountered a significant opponent in his skirmishes with the Hittites.

Seti and Ramses

Ramses received a good introduction to the Hittite problem, because he was "in the army" as a boy, though he did not actually come along during the campaigns of Year 5 and Year 6. By now he was in his early teens, and Seti appointed him a Commander in the army, eventually Commander-in-Chief. During this time, he gained valuable experience just as his father had with Ramses I. Since Ramses was physically strong, his father did not hesitate early in his reign to give him a title which made him heir-apparent: "Senior King's Son."

Ramses gained his first real battle experience in Seti's Year 5, when a new threat arose in the West. The Libyans decided to attack and a remarkable piece of evidence shows that Ramses might have fought. The war with Libya joins carvings of other battles on the walls at Karnak. We can see that the original design of this part omits Ramses, but that somebody later inserts him. That could even have been Ramses himself later when *he* was pharaoh.

Seti and the Hittites

About Year 6, Seti decided to attack the Hittites. This time he took Ramses along and headed for the city of Qadesh in northern Syria. He says quite specifically that he wanted to go "conquer Qadesh and the (Hittite) land of Amurru." As we might expect, the Hittites envisioned a different agenda. They were now led by a son of Shuppiluliuma named Mursilis.

The Hittites under Mursilis II had grown rusty, and when Seti and his troops filed over the horizon, the Hittites were unprepared. Seti found himself master of Qadesh, where the Egyptians had last set foot in the reign of his hero, Tuthmose III, around 150 years before. Seti left a joyful stele right in the city. As one could guess, it honored the god Amun, but it added Seth and Montu. The fascination of Ramses with these two began with his father.

Seti could now claim to have made a good start toward restoration of the empire of Tuthmose III. To his credit, he knew that this would not settle the matter and he seems to have reached a peace treaty with the new Hittite king, Muwatallis. Ramses saw this honorable solution and learned a valuable lesson, though it took him a while to digest it.

The victory at Qadesh sufficed to keep Seti I happy for the rest of his reign. The ensuing truce with the Hittites, which Ramses may not have approved of later, did give Seti the leisure for the other half of his program. Having echoed some of the achievements of Tuthmose III in the field, he could now aspire to emulate Amenhotep III in his new building program.

Seti's Turn to Build

That always takes us back to Karnak, to start with. Seti carried out the program here with great skill. The reliefs he left on the building rank with the finest work done there, and the conception of it has to be credited mainly to him and to Ramses I, though it was left for Ramses II to execute it.

Seti looked after the carvings of the northern end of the Hypostyle Hall. His subjects there were religious, showing the barges of Amun plying the Nile during the festival of Opet, and depicting parts of the rituals as they actually took place in the temple. The exterior at Karnak on the north depicts Seti in various battles, in Palestine, Syria, and Libya. It shows him "presenting" all this to Amun.

By this time, the pharaohs for a thousand years had sought sepulture in other ways than by building pyramids, so Seti had the workmen already busy with a fine tomb for him in the Valley of the Kings across the Nile, not far from the tomb of Ramses I, and tunnelled back into the cliff. The villagers of Deir el-Medina formed a permanent workforce there in Ramessid times, and found always enough employment available, with each pharaoh preparing his tomb as long

as he had time to. We have the village these people inhabited, and a wealth of information about them, including their names, which house each individual owned, the work-records, even the villagers' own tombs, which they took time to decorate nicely too. The tomb of Sennedjem in particular has furnished very useful information, and even a few of the objects in the Ramses Exhibit. So, they geared up on Seti's tomb, which fortunately he did not yet need.

With the tomb always goes a mortuary chapel. This need was to inspire Ramses II to one of his finest buildings (the Ramesseum), but meanwhile Seti got the men to work on his, using some of the same motifs he had employed at Karnak.

Abydos

The Ramessids exhibited a special devotion to the city of Abydos, a few miles down the Nile from Thebes. Here, we may recall, the wealthy class in the Twelfth Dynasty had located their tombs--some 800 of them known so far.

Seti wished to set up a temple here in the city of Osiris, father of Seth. Osiris was father too of Horus, who succeeded him, and became the prototype of all kings of Egypt. So in honoring both Seth and Osiris, as well as by taking Horus-names and ruling as heir of Horus, Seti carefully covered all theological eventualities.

What this leaves out is Isis, the mother of Horus and Seth. No surprise, therefore, to find her prominent in the corpus of paintings the dynasty left us, and she appears in Seti's tomb as his protectress.

The Twelfth Dynasty had reasserted royal control of Egypt after the First Intermediate Period, which threatened central government. They

126

had turned to Abydos because it symbolized the right of kings to rule firmly. When we find the early Ramessids here again, it is for the same reason. They had seen Akhnaton lose control, and they wanted to assert that the time had now come to heal the wounds.

In Abydos, Seti achieved one of the loveliest buildings in all Egypt, and its preservation has been remarkable. He used the finest limestone he could obtain, of a pure white that takes color well. His sculptors knew every line of their subjects, and the painters produced a marvellous harmony with the stone and the shapes. Colors here remain bright, not as brilliant as in some of the tombs at Thebes, but still as fresh as if done recently. The fine stone allowed a higher level of achievement than even at Thebes. The building is a masterpiece.

Seti enjoyed color. His buildings swim in it, and the palace he built up north in the Delta used white plaster with bright painted dadoes and with tiles, glazed in bright colors. Put the Egyptian sun on that place, and just stand back. Better was to come, too, when the "turquoise city" of Pi-Ramsese began to rise under Ramses II.

Seti at Work

We have a quarry inscription in which Seti claims to lie awake at night thinking up good things for his people and their gods, especially if he can obtain "excellent, hard sandstone" to build with.

To get ancient Egyptians working for you with the skill and zeal they did for him ranks as an achievement, and Seti knew one way to do it. All very well to inspire loyalty and to stir patriotism, but he knew that both armies and craftsmen work best when well-fed. Here's what his

nocturnal wakefulness produced on one occasion, in his own words. "His majesty increased the rations for the army of ointment, beef, and fish; he also gave vegetables without limit. Every man received four pounds of bread per day, with vegetables, roast meat, and two sacks of grain per month." Small wonder one inscription says, "They worked for His Majesty with a loving heart." (Kitchen, p. 26.)

This counted as one of the best times ever to be Egyptian, and the reign went on for sixteen years, with Ramses II yet to come.

Prelude to Ramses

One reason for the eventual success of the reign of Ramses II was the care his father took to groom him for the post. Ramses himself alludes to this in a formal address he made some years later. He says,

> I was just a youth in my father's embrace when he said, "Let him appear as king, so that I may behold his beauty while I'm still alive...Place the Great Crown on his head.
> He provided me a household from the Royal Harem...
> wives comparable to the beautiful ones from the Palace, and concubines raised in the Harem.

By the time Ramses came to the throne he already had over twenty children, a good thing, given the death and failure rate among Egyptian princes.

To echo the title his father held, *Men-ma-re* ("Abiding in Right is Re"), Ramses took the title *Usi-ma-re* ("Mighty in Right is Re").

Ramses was not the only one being prepared for power. Others in his family already had it. His sister, Tjia, was older than her brother,

CAMPAIGN TO CONQUER LAND OF KUSH

and she married early in his lifetime. She married Tia, son of Amen-wa-su. Tia took advantage of being son-in-law of the pharaoh, Seti, and became one of the Royal Scribes. His father became a Table-Scribe, an important post because it let him control the palace food-intake.

Ramessid Officialdom

We get an idea here of the detail of the Egyptian bureaucracy. Not the phony proliferation of offices we have with First Assistant Deputy Secretary and posts like that, but a carefully gradated, specific series of appointments. Thanks to the Egyptian habit of committing *everything* to writing, we can trace these people in detail.

Seti Searches the Southlands

In his Year 8, Seti made an expedition against a tribe in Kush, far to the south. He boasts in a monument set up by the Viceroy of Nubia, Amen-em-ope, and found down there, that he brought back the usual abundance of cattle and captives, but he seems proudest of seizing "six wells," which he proceeds to name. When he passed by Thebes on the way home, he decided not to interfere with the series of decorations at Karnak by interpolating this campaign, so he gave orders to change a few Canaanite names in the list to Nubian ones.

That capture of six "wells"--actually oases--put him in mind of the perennial water-problem in Upper Egypt and Nubia. This was

important, for the gold supply required systematic exploitation of the natural seams up there.

The next year, Year 9, he took a long trip in the Edfu desert, where the gold mountains lie. He left a narrative of his adventures. Its introductory words show him a man not overly careful regarding his health: "Year 9, third month of summer (June), day 20."

Somehow Seti survived. He says he stopped for rest, and started talking to himself (the sun will do that to you): "How hard is the waterless road!...Who shall quench our thirst? The (watered) land lies far away and the desert is wide." He asked help from Amun, Re, Ptah, and Osiris. They "showed" him where to dig, and "water...like the Nile floods at Aswan" was the reward. This theme recurs in the reign of Ramses.

Early Deeds of Ramses

Also in Year 9, he and Ramses found a new source of black granite in a quarry near Aswan, to go with red quartzite they had already. One of the first civil appointments for Ramses is recorded right on the rock here: "The Senior Son...did service to his majesty" making statues and obelisks, as well as barges for their transport.

Ramses began his career as soldier and as a supervisor of works before he took power, and he also started his great work as a builder then. His taste for spectacular monuments originated at his father's knee, so to speak, and we find him laboring on major buildings already in the last years of Seti's reign. He also began to take responsibility for dealing directly with the important ring of officials in place for this work.

Last Years of Seti

By Year 14, Seti had reached his early fifties. He ruled over an Egypt of restored stability, with borders secure and no real foreign enemies in the field, since the Hittites lay under treaty and the Nubians exhausted. Seti had begun a revival that he reflected in his superb building program, and his reforms lasted. His vigorous son partly accounts for that, and has overshadowed his father for posterity, but like a good parent, Seti made it all possible.

During the final years of Seti, Ramses appears more and more often in the record of Egyptian affairs. He had already begun his military career in a fledgling way, and in those years he took the increasing opportunities to demonstrate his mettle.

Egyptians always said the Nubians were revolting. If an open rebellion was not under way, a covert one could be alleged. So, just as Seti had given Ramses some early experience down there, so did Ramses now begin to take some of his own young sons into the field against puzzled Nubians.

His oldest boy was named Amen-hir-wonmef. He and his brother, Khaemwaset, appear in the record of a Nubian campaign when they were both just toddlers--four or five years old.

Peoples of the Sea

An important theatre of war for young Ramses developed in these pre-rule years. Hints occur of a new and potentially dangerous

movement, what came to be known as "The Peoples of the Sea." These were sometimes only pirates, but at other times we hear of what must be parts of migrating tribes. They appear for centuries along the coasts of the Aegean and Mediterranean Seas, and have been seen as the ancestors of the Palestinians, the Sardinians out west, the Sicilians, and others.

Records show them sweeping down on coastal regions of Asia Minor, where the Hittites tried to hold them back. They may have had a distant connection with the fall of Troy, which on some reconstructions occurred late in the lifetime of Ramses II. When they bounced off Asia Minor, they appeared in Cyprus, or on the coast of the Levant (from Syria southward), or they could even reach the Delta of Egypt.

That may have gone on intermittently for some time, and the worst attack came later, soon after 1200 B.C., during the reign of Ramses III. So the threat lay up there in the north all through the reign of Ramses II, and may have influenced the decision to build a new capital city in the Delta.

One of these raids occurred in the last years of Seti, While Ramses II was in his early twenties. He was deputed to meet them, and we have his own account of what happened.

The term he uses for these invaders is "Sherden," one of several tribal names employed over the centuries. Some scholars view the Sherden as the original settlers later of Sardinia, if one of these moving tribes deflected westward after rebounding off Egypt.

Ramses calls himself, "one who defeated the warriors of the sea...the unruly Sherden whom no one had ever known how to combat. They came boldly in warships from the midst of the sea, and none were able

to withstand them." But the mighty arm of pharaoh smote them and "the Delta now lies asleep."

The Royal Harems

The other preparation for rule, as mentioned before, was zealous attention to his royal harem. His harem in the Delta probably existed uncompromisingly for increasing his family's size and range.

The other harem, near the royal hunting and fishing grounds in the Fayum, appears more recreational. It also gave refuge, as we learn on several occasions, to queens or concubines who had passed childbearing age, or fallen from favor. On at least one occasion, a queen who had been sent there by Ramses re-emerged under his successor.

Even as a young man, Ramses already had his main wife, his favorite, Nefertari. She's the one called "Great Queen" for the early part of his reign, though something may have gone wrong later.

Also in this early period Ramses had a second wife, not the favorite but destined to become so. This was Istnofret, about whom surprisingly little is known, though some of her children can be distinguished.

Between them, the two women gave him several children, including the oldest son, Amen-hir-wonmef, by Nefertari, and a little Ramses by Istnofret. Nefertari was the mother of the fourth daughter, Meryetamun and of several sons, including Pre-hir-wonmef and all the way down to the sixteenth son, Mery-Atum. Istnofret also had the fourth son, our old friend Khaemwaset ("Appearing in Thebes").

Istnofret produced Ramses' first daughter, who has the strange name of Bint-Anath, that is, "daughter of Anath." Anath is a Syrian

LIFE IN ANCIENT EGYPT

In Ancient Egypt musicians entertained at banquets. These women play the harp, lute, and flute.

goddess, and it's interesting to see in this name another example of the favor Ramses showed to Syrians, as if trying to detach them in this manner from the Hittites.

Istnofret also produced Merenptah, who was the thirteenth son, but destined to be the successor of Ramses. Not surprisingly, the major wives produced the major children. (Details on these: Kitchen, p. 39 f.)

Isis

Hathor

136

Chapter 6

Ramses Rules
and Fights
at Qadesh

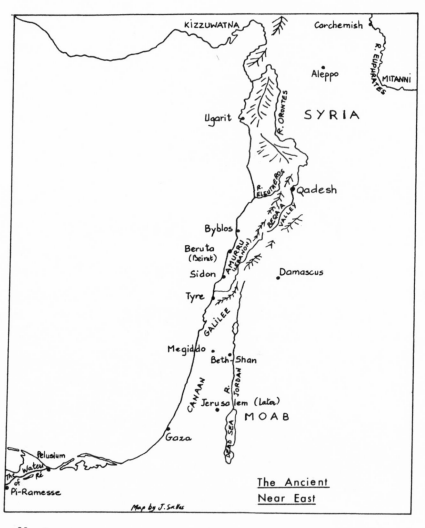

KIZZUWATNA

Carchemish

R. EUPHRATES

Aleppo

MITANNI

Ugarit

R. ORONTES

SYRIA

R. ELEUTHEROS

Qadesh

BEQAA VALLEY

Byblos

AMURRU (LEBANON)

Beruta (Beirut)

Sidon

Damascus

Tyre

GALILEE

Megiddo

Beth-Shan

CANAAN

R. JORDAN

Jerusalem (Later)

MOAB

Gaza

DEAD SEA

Pelusium

The Waters of Ré

Pi-Ramesse

The Ancient
Near East

Map by J. Salles

No. 4

The New Pharaoh, Ramses II

For those who require a precise date, Ramses became pharaoh in 1304, 1290 or 1279. The problem here is that although the reign is solidly fixed at 67 years, one can't readily say when they ran. We can choose amongst the most likely, depending on the reigns of other kings or on certain astronomical phenomena. Whole books are available on the question. (See Bibliography:*CAH* I, 1, 189; Kitchen; Schmidt.)

Ramses is titled *Usi-ma-re,* "Strong in Right is Re." He adds another epithet, *"The Chosen One of Re."* His other two titles are *Meri-Amun,* "Beloved of Amun," and then his name, *Ra-mes-ses,* "Child of Re."

Why this comparative weight on Re? Various explanations come to mind, especially when one inspects the map. Re was localized, like most Egyptian gods. He was especially associated with the town of Heliopolis, "City of the Sun" (ancient Egyptian *Iunu,* the biblical *On*).

That was about as far north as you could go and still find a main-stream god. It lies north even of Memphis, and just at the edge of the Delta. Not too surprisingly, it's the closest major god's sanctuary to Tanis and Avaris, where the family of Ramses originated.

The only major god closer to home for them would be Seth, and one dared not make *him* the patron god. The populace would rise in outrage if Ramses put this belligerent, evil-minded, foreign-sounding god too high in the state.

The other motive lay in respect for the dangerous priesthood of Amun, the rival sun-god of Thebes, at the other end of Egypt. Ramses had little liking for Amun, and rightly feared any shift of power in that direction, as had occurred in the past and later did again, to the detriment of the Ramessids. When Ramses stresses that he is son of

Re, he vaults all the way back to the pharaohs of pyramid times, who voyaged with Re every night. Ramses yearned to preside over a mighty state as they had, and he brought it to pass.

His royal titles clarify his intentions. Besides those names and the title "Son of Re" he carefully adds "Beloved of Amun." He can already call himself "Great in Victories" and "Protector of Egypt." He adds that he "restrains the foreigners" and of course he is "Mighty Bull."

The Funeral of Seti I

Ramses had seventy days to wait before the body of his father could complete the traditional rites of embalming. He used at least part of the time in planning his new city, right in the Delta near home, in the vicinity of Avaris. He declared its name early on: Pi-Ramesse A-nakhtu, "The City of Ramses, Great-of-Victories."

By late August of his first regnal year, he was on the way upriver with the mummy. This was an incredible sight for ancient Egyptians, lining the Nile's banks to watch the royal barques under full sail upstream. The great ceremony took place that way for thousands of years. Now it was Seti's turn.

The procession stopped at Heliopolis to reassure Re, and proceeded to Memphis for further recognition of the new king, with a bow toward another powerful god, Ptah. Then upstream past the pyramids for hours on end, past the Fayum and the ancient cities of Middle Egypt, probably stopping at Abydos.

Finally, the flotilla reached Thebes. Besides ceremonies at Karnak and Luxor, this area demanded attention as it contained the memorial

temple of Seti, constructed for this occasion and for centuries to follow. Here Ramses officially became Horus, charged with burying his father, Osiris. Then followed burial in the vast tomb that Seti had constructed in the Valley of the Kings. Ramses now sealed it.   He would eventually be interred in this tomb when a flash flood destroyed his own magnificent tomb.

Ramses Rules Alone

In Turin, Italy, one of the finest statues remaining of Ramses probably dates to this initial period of his reign. It depicts him as a full pharaoh, holding regalia of office. He wears the pharaonic head-dress, the *khepresh,* with the *uraeus* cobra in front for protection. He also wears the *wesekh* collar.

Ramses began the religious exercises of his reign shrewdly. The great yearly festival of Opet approached in September, while he was there, so he took full advantage. Like so many of these things, the festival consisted mainly of donning full regalia and perambulating solemnly in the god's vicinity.

Egyptians added a typical flavor of their own to all this. Since the Nile loomed large in their thinking, they contrived whenever they could to get a boat-trip for the god into the ceremonies. (The famous Cleopatra began her reign 1300 years later by claiming that she and her brother helped row a sacred bull, the Buchis, across the Nile near here.)

Ramses officiated. That meant a trip for the god from Karnak to Luxor. Amun stayed in Luxor for about three weeks, and this time so did Ramses, probably poking about the widespread construction work he had in prospect there. At the end of the period, Amun was taken on

board and was transported the two miles back.

For Ramses, this accomplished necessary stroking of the powerful priesthood of Amun there in Thebes. Without their support, he might have a wobbly reign, but now they could recall how he opened his tenure of office among them.

Returning North

Ramses took the opportunity for another kind of political initiation. He appointed a large contingent of new priests and officers. As part of this process, the royal entourage turned back for northern Egypt. An eyewitness describes it: "Year One...Beginning the journey, setting sail, the royal ships illuminating the waters, turning northwards...His Majesty turned aside to see his Father (Osiris), traversing the waters of the Abydos canal..." (Kitchen, p. 45.)

A few miles downstream they pulled in to the right bank of the river and went ashore. This was Abydos, the city sacred to Osiris where some kings had been buried from at least the first dynasty. By no accident, Seti I and Ramses II chose Abydos for their great king-list, the "Canon of Abydos," depicting the cartouches of no fewer than 76 royal predecessors.

The concern of Ramses for the graves of these early kings re-emphasizes his regard for continuity; in this lay his hope for a "legitimate" and stable dynasty. This city fittingly also now enjoyed, through Ramses and his father, a marvellous series of buildings, with some of the loveliest painting ever done in Egypt.

New Appointments

The new appointments by Ramses have left vivid traces here. Evidence comes from the very tomb of one official involved. (West Thebes, Tomb 157. See Kitchen, pp. 46 ff.) It affords an unusual glimpse of Ramses at work. The official, Neb-wen-enef, has carved a representation of the scene as it took place; this doubtless came as the high point of his own life.

Ramses is shown in the Window of Appearance of the palace in Abydos. His favorite queen, Nefertari, leans in just behind him. The new priest of Amun, previously designated in Thebes, has come down and now formally receives the appointment. He has left as well a full account of what was done.

> Year one, third month of the inundation. His Majesty sailed north after doing the pleasure of Amun-Re, with Mut and Khons (the Theban triad), in the beautiful Festival of Opet. Neb-wen-enef came into his presence... His Majesty said, 'You are now the High Priest of Amun! You are chief over his domain, his foundations, his treasure, his granary. (Vast wealth in all this.) Your *son* now takes over the priesthood you formerly had of Hathor, Lady of Dendera, inheriting the place of his *ancestors* (emphasis mine)."

Remarkable evidence here of how these priesthoods remained in one noble family for generations, creating a stable and predictable tradition of office.

The inscription continues, "His Majesty gave him two signet-rings and an electrum staff of office." The man also inherits a strong workforce of all the craftsmen in Thebes. Ramses in the ceremony calls himself "Amun's Ruler" to ensure that Neb-wen-enef doesn't forget where this all came from.

Abydos

In Abydos, Ramses discovered one shocking situation, quite common in Egypt despite the constant pressure against it. This was neglect.

Ramses says, "The cemetery *belonging to former kings* (emphasis mine) in Abydos was falling into ruin...one brick not touching the next. What was barely begun had mouldered...No son renewed a father's monument." And, "Even the temple of *Men-ma-re* (throne name of Seti I) was unfinished, front and rear, with pillars not set onto the terrace. The statue lay on the ground not fashioned in accord with the regulations of the Sacred Workshop...Divine offerings had ceased; so had the priests. The field produce was lost since the boundaries were not properly marked out."

Ramses also said, "I am determined to confer benefits on my father such that it will be said ever after that his son perpetuated his name..." Then Ramses gave orders to "every grade of craftsman" by way of the Chief of Works, and soldiers, sculptors, and workmen to "restore what was ruined in the cemetery."

144

The Gods Again

Thebes and Abydos formed a gateway to Nubia, where he had spent time and would again. Military and trade matters brought him there, but so did the lure of gold. To secure the region ranked high among the priorities of any pharaoh. Thebes enjoyed high prestige as the seat of Amun; and his priesthood. It ranked high for other reasons as well, and we know Ramses appreciated them. Here's what he says about the locale during his third regnal year.

> His Majesty did research in the office of archives. He opened the writings of the House of Life. He learned the secrets of heaven and the mysteries of earth. He found Thebes, the very Eye of Re, to be *the original plot of earth which arose in the beginning, since this land has existed.* (Emphasis mine.) At that time, Amun-Re existed as king--he illumined heaven and shone upon the sun's circuit, to where his Eye's rays might fall.

He then stresses the two domains of the sun, here in Thebes and up north in Heliopolis.

The story of the Flood was current throughout the East, and even in Greece. A possible interpretation of this passage would show that Thebes had managed to claim its place as the first piece of earth to emerge after the Flood, or from the sea in more distant geological times when land was formed from primeval slime.

Ramses tried not to step on theological toes, but had to respect Thebes, however much he disliked it and its claims.

Ramses and the Gold Supply

In his third year, Ramses decided to put his throne on a more solid foundation. "Money talks," and nothing props up a throne better than gold. Ramses moved to get more, realizing that this was a crucial need.

His Majesty was sitting on the electrum throne (a rare amalgam of silver and gold), wearing the head-fillet and tall plumes. He was pondering the desert, where gold lay, and planning wells along the route... There is much gold in the desert of Akuyati, but the road is waterless. Only half of a gold expedition will survive--they and their donkeys perish.

A message from the viceroy of Nubia arrived to announce that a well dug by Seti I went 180 feet and came in dry. People are dying of thirst. The viceroy intoned, "If *you* say, to your father the Nile god, 'Let water flow' (it will)." He then told them to go, and where to dig. "Water appeared at twelve cubits (18 feet)!" People reacted with predictable enthusiasm: "The very waters of the underworld listen to Ramses!....He is the god Thoth himself."

The Campaigns of Ramses

Ramses probably thought his father should *not* have made peace with the Hittites, since he had to give up traditional Egyptian claims to do so. As soon as Ramses acquired his own opportunity, he set out to achieve military reknown.

By Year 4, he took the road to Syria. Canaan had been recovered by Seti and had not since fallen away, so this part of the trip passed smoothly. He reached a point near Tyre and Byblos on the Lebanese coast, and he took some of the inland cities by siege.

That allowed him to move into the Syrian area known as *Amurru,* where the Egyptians and the Hittites *both* had claims. It had supposedly become a free state, with a king called Benteshina. Benteshina strikes the observer as a prudent man. He hastily offered to send Ramses all the tribute he wished, and he received in turn reconfirmation of his throne.

That meant he had to inform his former overlord, the Hittite monarch Muwatallis, that he'd be serving Ramses now, since he hadn't received adequate protection from the Hittites.

Muwatallis spent that winter preparing for what proved one of the most famous battles of ancient history.

The Battle of Qadesh

Like most wars, this one might have been avoided. Five years before, when the Hittite king, Muwatallis, learned that Ramses had just come to the throne, he sent a prince from North Syria as envoy to Egypt, announcing his happiness. Relations remained calm, at first. But one does not become a great conqueror without great victories, and that had to mean Hittites, in the world of Ramses' time.

On both sides the forces began to organize. Hittites always demonstrated a talent for assembling tribes of allies into vast confederacies. They now commenced, according to a contemporary account, to "collect all the foreign lands as far as the ends of the ocean"--the "entire Hittite land, and Nahrin," with the Syrian and

Anatolian rulers from Kizzuwatna, Qode, Arvad, Nuhashshe, Ugarit, Aleppo, Carchemish, Qadesh. The tribes included these, the Kezweden, the Pedes and others.

Altogether, Muwatallis levied forces from sixteen regions as well as the Hittite homeland. One count gives 2500 chariots and a double army which totalled 37,000 men, though some estimates go as low as 20,000. Muwatallis even hired some interesting mercenaries-- occupants of what became the Greek lands of Asia Minor: Lycians, Mysians, Cilicians, Dardanians.

Ramses began to collect allies of his own, but Egypt couldn't draw on anything like the assemblage the Hittites could. He rummaged up a few Nubians, and had the Syrian garrisons of "Sherden," and probably some Meshwesh from Libya. But mainly he relied on recruits from Egypt, many of them from the standing army. He may have got together a total of 20,000 men as well.

Whether outnumbered or not, Ramses confidently set off northward in April of "Year 5." Ramses records that he "began the march well, in Year 5, second month of summer, day 9...being powerful like Montu... (and) all the foreign lands trembled before him." People remembered to pay their tax arrears. He brought along several sons and family members.

The route they took led through Gaza, Canaan, and Galilee into Lebanon. Ramses exulted at the thought of following the path blazed for him by the great Egyptian conquerors of the Eighteenth Dynasty, especially Thutmose III, 150 years before.

Ramses divided his army along religious lines. He employed four main divisions, named for Amon, Re, Ptah and Seth. It is a decided advantage to assure men about to die that they're doing it for god.

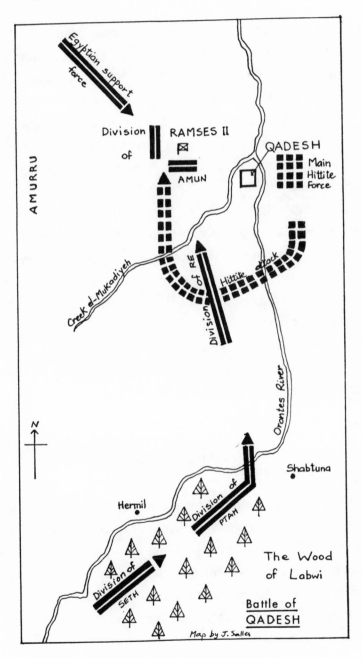

Battle of
__QADESH__

Map by J. Salles

No. 5

Historians and novelists (recently, Norman Mailer in *Ancient Evenings*) get great mileage out of campaigns like this one. Ramses did too. People enjoyed the drama of Ramses in his glittering chariot sweeping steadily northward, hacking away at the enemy in Beth Shan, Megiddo, Dog River. He reached the lower Orontes River, the important one you see on the maps of Syria sweeping upward in an arc between the mountain ranges until it enters the sea near ancient Antioch in the north.

Whoever follows this river to Syria from Palestine must pass Qadesh. Ramses knew it and the Hittites knew it. We've seen in our own day the importance of this region--the Beqa'a Valley especially. Ramses remembered the successes of Thutmose III and of his own father here, and determined to echo them. Muwatallis held a differing opinion on the matter.

A month after leaving Egypt, Ramses camped at last on a ridge from which the vast plain surrounding Qadesh lay visible. In the distance, the city beckoned him on to glory. He saw and exulted.

The Con

Ramses swept down into the plain and moved across it. For several days his scouts had been reporting that no Hittites appeared anywhere. Two Beduin ("Shosu") came up to him and declared that they had deserted from the composite forces of the Hittites. They waved beyond the horizon toward Aleppo, about 100 miles northeast, and said that the Hittites had withdrawn there out of apprehension over the size and grandeur of Ramses' army. The young pharaoh believed this story and

acted accordingly.

The glory of entering Qadesh would fall to him on the morrow, he reflected with keen expectation while advancing steadily toward it. He left three of his divisions east of the Orontes River, in the wood called Labwi, and with the fourth, the Amun division, he crossed over at the ford near Shabtuna (Ribleh). Thus a classic error right at the start. The other divisions were to catch up slowly, and Re crossed next, leaving Ptah and Seth behind, on the far side of the river. (Breasted, Chapter XXI, gives an excellent account of this battle, and devoted a book to it: *The Battle of Kadesh,* Chicago 1903. A good modern bibliography: Kitchen p. 249.)

The Set-Up

Muwatallis had not withdrawn to Aleppo at all; he lay near Qadesh. The Hittite force had moved to a point east of the river, out of sight of the Egyptians coming up the west side. The Hittites carefully advanced southward on their side as Ramses advanced northward on his. When Egyptians looked toward Qadesh, the Hittites lay always *behind* it. The perspective changed constantly as Ramses and his forces pressed onward.

Ramses halted about six miles northwest of the city, on the same side of the river, near the little stream called El-Mukadiyeh. The Hittites remained out of sight on the other side. The Re division straggled on toward Ramses and his Amun division, while Ptah and Seth had not even crossed the river yet. Ramses had halted for the day, or so he thought.

About now, two Hittite scouts were brought in, captured by the

Egyptians. After the usual courtesies--cunning tortures--they were hustled before Ramses.

> His Majesty said, 'Who are you?' They replied, 'We belong to the ruler of Hatti. He sent us to look for you.' 'Where is he, then? I heard he was at Aleppo, north of Tunip.' 'Au contraire, Master; he and his sea of allies are ready to fight, just over there behind the Old Quarter of Qadesh.'

This focused upon them the full attention of young Ramses in a manner few things did. He wasted some precious time berating his officers. He also sent the royal family to safety, led by one of the princes, Pre-hir-wonmef. By then he could see the Re division approaching in the distance, too far away to help him or for him to join. He sent an urgent message to Ptah to cross the Orontes immediately and join them.

The Sting

Meanwhile, the Hittites began to re-cross the river, right between Ramses and those other two divisions of his army, Ptah and Seth. The Hittites in fact landed right where the division of Re was still plodding northward, weary. Re got the Experience of their lives. The Hittite chariots rode straight through them, scattering the division like quail. One knot of men escaped intact, and fled northward.

When Ramses and the troops of Amun looked up, here came these remnants of Re, crashing into the camp's new rampart, with the Hittites about two jumps behind. The whole mess rolled up into a ball

of misery, with Ramses somewhere in the middle. The rest of Ramses' army still lay the other side of the Orontes, with 2500 Hittite chariots in between, and a vast Hittite foot-army over there somewhere too. Ramses decided he had better make a plan.

Here's where fate and the individual combine to earn either a footnote in history or a chapter. Ramses had with him only his officers, some of his retinue, and his palace guard. But he had his four-horse chariot, and he had been born and bred a pharaoh.

Ramses later records an inspired speech he now gave to an audience of one, his shield-bearer, Menna: "I shall go for them like a falcon!" The Amun division meanwhile had hastily retreated in a northerly direction and the Re division had achieved a remarkable state of disarray. Ramses had to "go it alone," he later maintained.

The Battle

He noticed that the Hittites were surrounding him from the south. They had all the room in the world to do that toward the west, but on the east they had to squeeze in between Ramses and the river. He saw that this meant a thin line for them, so he charged.

That so startled the Hittites that some fell into the river. Ramses liked that and tried again, mentally keeping track of the splashes.

Now when you're concentrating on chariots to the east of you, then those to the west of you are behind your back. Most men fight better in the front. Ramses turned his back on the larger enemy, and lived. Why? Because the Hittites to the west of him had by now encountered the baggage-trains, always a delicious moment in an ancient battle, especially when the goodies belong to a pharaoh. They probably had

never seen such treasures, and were already stuffing it into their robes, counting up their black-market earnings.

Lady Luck

Luck enters into battles, too. About five weeks before, Ramses had sent an auxiliary force along the coast, and told them to turn inland in Syria and meet him at Qadesh. This force arrived just in time to catch the Hittites absorbed in looting. Ramses stayed out in the river whaling stragglers. The looters fell or fled. Things were looking up.

Meanwhile, the division of Amun had stopped running north and found nobody was chasing it. So it turned around and made the camp just in time to help Ramses clean up. From the south, another bit of help arrived. The division of Ptah had crossed the river and wandered northward. It now arrived, late in the afternoon. The Hittites thereupon found themselves in a vice, with Amun and Re above and Ptah below.

It seems that the Hittite infantry still remained west of the river, where the Seth division of Egyptians were too. So, no diversion there. The Hittites had only one choice: the chariots withdrew into Qadesh! If you can't defend a city, then hide in it.

Day Two

Ramses and his men looked at one another with new wisdom and slight exophthalmia, yesterday's early cockiness long-since vanished

from their stunned visages. To be sure, in years to come, Ramses was to portray Day One as an unmitigated success. He festooned the walls at Abu Simbel, Karnak, Luxor, the Ramesseum, Abydos and probably Pi-Ramesse with scenes of himself calmly dealing justice to a host of supplicants. He even enjoyed a little joke now and then, as in a famous scene from the Ramesseum, where the retainers have to hold the enemy Prince of Aleppo upside-down to empty him of river-water.

What Ramses didn't dwell on, though it emerges from his pictures and narrative, was that the Hittites had taught the world a lesson. Their advance across the river from concealment behind Qadesh constituted the first deliberate flanking movement known in military history, and it nearly enveloped Ramses. Only the lack of discipline shown by the Hittite charioteers on the western flank kept the maneuver from succeeding, and the timely arrival of the contingent from the coast could not have been foreseen by the Hittites, though their scouts should have picked up the approach of a large body of men there.

Now, Ramses was not a "team player." Here's part of his official version of the battle.

> The army came to praise me, seeing what I had done.
> (I said) '...you deserted me; I was left alone. Not
> an officer or captain or soldier assisted as I battled.
> I fought untold numbers of foreign contingents. Only
> two remained with me, named Victory in Thebes and Mut
> is Content--and they were my chariot horses! They only.
> From now on I will personally feed them!' (Full version
> in Kitchen, pp. 60-61.)

The Egyptians had survived, but had suffered enormous losses, especially from Amun and Re, with considerable damage to Ptah. The

155

Seth division never did get into battle and remained fresh, but who dared rely on *it*? In addition, everyone suddenly realized in the battle's aftermath that the army lay that night 250 miles from home, in a sea of hostile armed men. Ramses grew thoughtful.

Across the Orontes, Muwatallis found that he had lost a number of his army commanders, lead charioteers, shield bearers, and troops. Two of his royal brothers had also perished, along with the chief of his personal guard.

Hittites usually preferred to use diplomacy when the opportunity existed. The policy had served them well for centuries throughout their vast realm and its disparate lands. More than a decade before, Muwatallis had achieved a formal accord with Egypt, during the reign of Ramses' father. He now sent messengers to Ramses suggesting they brush off the dust and call it even.

Ramses had the wit to consult his commanders, who replied with one voice, "Peace is good, O Majesty and Sovereign!" No need to draw *them* a diagram of the position.

Accordingly, the two parties concluded an informal truce, providing for the status quo as before the battle. That basically let Ramses off the hook, and allowed him to return home a hero. As soon as he was over the horizon, Muwatallis began to reoccupy most of what Ramses had taken on the way to Qadesh, and of course he retained the city itself.

What Ramses did gain ranked far higher than the terrritory concerned: he could now with some veracity boast that he had bearded the Hittite in his den and lived to tell of it. The ultimate issue remained to be settled, but back home few at first realized that, and not one of them found it expedient to mention this perception.

LIFE IN ANCIENT EGYPT

In Ancient Egypt every town had an organization of women who hired out as professional mourners. They were paid to wail over the body of the departed one.

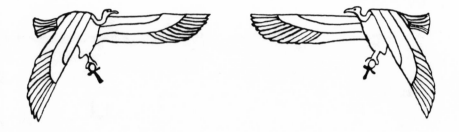

Chapter 7

The Subsequent Reign of Ramses

Ramses' Royal Cartouche

The Subsequent Reign of Ramses

In the vigorous years to follow, Ramses took the field many times more, pursuing the traditional policy of controlling Nubia, keeping the Libyans at bay, and attempting conquests in Lebanon and Syria. Ramses has been criticized for the twenty or so years of unnecessary fighting he engaged in with the Hittites especially, since an early pact with them appears to have been possible. (Kitchen, pp. 232 ff., summarizes the range of views regarding Ramses; cf. the more general treatment of Montet, Ch. 10, "Egypt as Seen by the Ancients and in the Light of Modern Research." The remainder of his reign *CAH* II, 2, ed. 3, pp. 229-232.)

Suffice it to say that Ramses did in fact achieve a full-fledged treaty with the Hittites, in "year 21," one that provided badly-needed stability to the ancient Near East for decades at a critical time in its history. Not surprisingly, the silver tablets originally carrying the text have not come down to us, but we have engraved on stone the text of this treaty in both Egyptian and Hittite-cuneiform versions.

These demonstrate how carefully both rulers had rooted it in the traditions of their two countries. The "thousand gods" of each not only witness the pact but guarantee enforcement of it. "Brotherhood" will prevail, as in all documents of the kind among Hittites. Neither side will engage in aggression against the other or permit outside parties to do so. Neither will harbor fugitives from the other's territory. (Details: Kitchen, pp. 75-81. Hittite policies: O.R. Gurney, *The Hittites,* Penguin 1952; 1954, pp. 76 ff.)

The provisions of this agreement strike us as familiar because they have been echoed so many hundreds of times in subsequent millennia,

but we must remember its extreme antiquity. It may well constitute the first treaty of its kind in history, though the preceding centuries of war and peace in Mesopotamia could have produced archetypes now lost. In any case, this far more than Qadesh ranks as the crowning achievement of Ramses in international affairs, with due credit as well to the Hittite monarch, Hattusilis III. So great was the impression made by this in antiquity, that one view of the Louvre's "Bentresh Stele" of about 300 B.C. sees it as inspired by these unprecedented arrangements between Ramses and the Hittites. (See Kitchen, p. 228.)

Details of the remaining political and military achievements of Ramses lie beyond the scope of this introduction to him. His wars, details of his administration of the kingdom, and the personnel through whom he worked have been treated in detail by others. (Notable among these is Kitchen, in Parts II-III; for others see bibliography. Also useful are the sections as cited herein of the revised *Cambridge Ancient History.*)

It remains to see the progress of his family, the great buildings through which he enriched posterity, and the new impetus he gave Egypt.

The Family

We must look now at the full development of Ramses' family. The partial family tree provided by Kitchen (p. 244) deliberately sets forth only a fraction of the "output" Ramses achieved in this regard. Estimates of Ramses' own progeny range upward from 100 sons and

LIFE IN ANCIENT EGYPT

In Ancient Egypt the Pharoah began his day with a visit to the barber. Women usually wore their hair in long arrangements of fine plaits; men sometimes wore wigs.

70 known daughters. The total must have been considerably higher, especially of daughters, when we take into account his early start, his great number of queens and concubines, and the long life he enjoyed. For over two hundred years, the "Ramessids" boasted descent from him and assumed high station in Egypt.

Nefertari

Of all the members of this great family, none rivals in renown the first major queen of Ramses. Her fame rests in part on her widespread depictions with him, and in part on her extant tomb. The major ingredient seems to be her great beauty, almost lovingly depicted on temple walls from Abu Simbel northward, and especially striking in her own extant tomb, now usually closed to protect its marvellous paintings. Nefertari is prominent at Abu Simbel, not only with her own chapel and the striking nude statue out among the colossi, but also pictured carefully on the walls. (E.g., Kitchen, p. 101.)

She joins Ramses on the walls of Luxor, spectacularly crowned, standing nearly as high as he is. (*Ramses le Grand*, p. xxii.) At Abydos, she joined him already in Year One at the installation of a new high-priest of Amun, and stands with Ramses in the Window of Appearance during the ceremony. She must have been shown in virtually all of his early monuments, and in many now lost at Pi-Ramesse.

Above all, we have her splendid tomb in the Valley of the Queens, remarkable for its high proportion of paintings to text, as if her beauty spoke for itself. The consistency of the depictions argues for portraits-

QUEEN NEFERTARI

from-life, and her fine partly diaphanous linen garments leave no doubt of her high station.

In the paintings, she surrounds herself with gods, many of whom she serves. She offers wine to Hathor. She is visited by Re-Harakhti and Amentit, goddess of the west. She appears with Isis. Osiris is there, with distinctive green face, looking as if he has swallowed too many snails. The god Atum of Heliopolis attends.

Nefertari appears throughout in attitudes of great devotion, carrying offerings or engaged in prayer, kneeling gracefully or standing before the gods. Her earthly life is not neglected here either, and once she appears with Ramses near the herd of cattle she can use for eternity.

The Paris Ramses exhibition of 1976 fittingly included a fine "reconstitution photographique de la tombe de Nofretari" and it proved one of the most popular items there. (*Ramses le Grand,* pp. 207-221.)

Istnofret

As discussed above, Ramses sired children from two queens in particular, first Nefertari, the "Great Queen" of his youth, and then Istnofret, who held the same title. A statue of her in the Louvre shows her with two of the children, Khaemwaset and the younger Ramses. An acephalic statue in Cairo may depict her as well, with a royal prince. (*Ramses le Grand,* xv and p. 75.)

Her relative obscurity now as compared to Nefertari stems partly from chronological factors. The enthusiastic celebrations Ramses bestowed on Nefertari in his initial years left reduced room later for

QUEEN NEFERTARI PLAYING CHESS

representations of Istnofret on some of the major monuments. Subsequent loss must be considered as well, but it seems likely that Nefertari outshone her rival in all that was done, just as she does all that survives.

Meryetamun

The first daughter produced by Nofretari, and fourth daughter for Ramses, was Meryetamun, who has now been identified by a large statue found at Akhmin in Upper Egypt in 1981. This in turn permits attribution to her of the lovely statue found in the Ramesseum in 1896. (Montreal no. 28; *Ramses le Grand* no. xiv., pp. 72-74.) The new statue terms her Great Royal Wife. She may have replaced her mother, in this rank; the older queen seems to have been demoted before her own death. But Meryetamun is here called "eldest daughter," which does not accord with other evidence about her position unless the previous three were now dead. Bint Anath is elsewhere termed the eldest. (See Montreal no. 28 on this.)

Meryetamun holds titles which her mother had held. She's the Superior of the Harem of Amun-Re. She's described as one

> ...with the splendid face, magnificent in the palace...
> When she opens her mouth to soothe the Lord of the
> Two Lands, one is satisfied with what is said.

She wears a skin-tight robe and carries the *menat,* a long pallette with a woman's head and ending in a rosette which supposedly represents the uterus. Only women carry it, usually at important gender-related moments: birth announcement, betrothal, marriage. The necklace displays *nefer* drops, elegant little symbols, in this case of beauty and youth.

Meryetamun's head-dress flares out from her forehead, merging smoothly with a double head-band carrying not one but two uraeus cobras. One of these wears the crown of Upper Egypt, one of Lower. The head-dress peaks in a ring of erect serpents topped by sun-disks. This sumptuous costume fully reflects the high position of this young woman, who appears about fourteen years of age as depicted.

Ramses II may have married her about this age, since she carries the menat. In any case, she did become Great Queen.

Khaemwaset

Her half-brother was Khaemwaset ("Appearing in Thebes"). (Kitchen, p. 103 f.) He was the fourth son, and Istnofret his mother. Oddly, he became the most famous of the children of Ramses II. He was interested in theology and literature; in fact, he became a priest of Ptah.

Khaemwaset helped build the new Serapeum, and is duly depicted on its walls with Ramses II. He helped in the search for a new Apis bull in year 16, and managed the search for its successor in year 30. He is credited with building a Temple of the Apis, with an extant inscription: "the gods have images here wrought in the Mansions of Gold." He was still associated in people's minds with the Apis cult some 1300 years later.

Like Ramses, Khaemwaset believed strongly in restoring the old monuments. He worked on the Great Pyramid, on the Step-Pyramid of Zoser at Saqqara, the Pyramid of Unas, and on numerous tombs.

He left inscriptions identifying each monument's owner and mentioning restoration by Ramses II and himself.

Khaemwaset superintended the Jubilees of Ramses as well. But he died in year 55. His tomb was discovered by Mariette in 1852. For centuries, Egyptians referred some of their stories and myths to him, "in the days of Khaemwaset."

Amun-hir-khopshef

Amun-hir-khopshef was the eldest son, by Nefertari, and it is instructive to see Ramses naming him not for his own favorite god, but for the Theban Amun, whom Ramses honored by the first act of his reign in attending the Opet festival there. About the same time, Ramses II gave his first son this name, meaning "Amun is with his strong arm." He also made him "Senior King's Son," just as he himself had been under Seti, and engaged in the usual range of activities expected of vigorous pharaohs, including a duck-hunt depicted with the usual vividness. (Kitchen, p. 34.)

Ramses appears on one relief with his oldest son in pursuit of a wild bull, which Amun-hir-khopshef has boldly but perhaps unwisely seized by the tail, while Ramses builds a loop in his leather lasso. With recreation such as this, the family might almost welcome battles against mere humans. (Photograph: *Ramses le Grand*, p. xxvi.)

Amun-hir-khopshef soon became "General-in-Chief" and the presumptive heir of Ramses. He fought in the Qadesh campaign, like the rest of the first fourteen sons; since he is not the one named as leading the family to safety during the Hittite attack, he was

presumably engaged with the enemy. He participated in the Moab campaign too, in year 7.

However, by year 20 he was no longer the heir-apparent, and must have been dead. His tomb exists in the Valley of the Queens, showing him with Isis, and behind him the feather of Maat. When Anubis leads him into the underworld, he's dressed in the regalia of a pharaoh-- which he didn't get the chance to become.

Other Sons

We have glimpses of others among the wide progeny of Ramses. His fifth son, Montu-hir-kopshef, or "Montu is with his strong right arm," has left a tomb. His portrait there as he offers to the gods shows him still young, in the early twenties at the oldest. The dark, prominent eyes and large lips characteristic of Ramses suggests a portrait typically faithful to life. (Photograph: Romer, *Ancient Lives,* no. 30.) He came to share the position of "First Charioteer of His Majesty" with the third son, one of Nefertari's, Pre-hir-wonmef, "Re is on his right hand." (Egyptians had no patience with "southpaws," whom the Romans regarded as positively *sinister,* their word for "left-handed.")

Bint-Anath

Finally, one other daughter needs mention, Bint-Anath, referred to earlier. She's named for a Syrian goddess and seems to have been a

favorite with Ramses. She apparently succeeded her mother, Istnofret, as Great Queen. This was after the death of Istnofret, and was not a replacement while living, as may have happened to Nefertari.

It has been suggested that the small figure standing between the feet of a colossus of Ramses before Pylon II at Karnak may be Bint-Anath. (Baines and Malek, pp. 92-93.) She served for a time as Queen and then retired into the harem, but she reappeared as a consort to Merneptah when he succeeded Ramses. (Kitchen, pp. 99 f., 110, 252 f.)

Other Queens

Nefertari, Istnofret, Meryetamun, and Bint-Anath by no means completed the roster of major queens of Ramses, and in addition his number of harem-ladies must have been very high. (Kitchen, p. 253.)

The Hittite Queen

One of the most spectacular additions to his retinue in this regard was Maat-hor-neferure, the *Hittite!* By year 34, when she was brought to the Egyptian court, Ramses had achieved the remarkable nonaggression pact with the Hittites. She came to him after a careful series of arrangements by the Hittites, but so eager were both sides for this marriage that her long journey down from Asia Minor fell in winter. Ramses prayed to the gods for fair weather, and suddenly "summer occurred in winter" during her progression southward. (Kitchen, pp. 83-89; 110; 229.)

The new queen, "daughter of the Great Ruler of Hatti," became "one fair of features, first among women...a very goddess" to the wide-eyed bridegroom. Glimpses of her accompanying him about the palace, receiving rolls of cloth, or endlessly celebrated on monuments by Ramses do give way to the inevitable picture of her sent into the harem during her later years. However, the memory of this unprecedented marriage (and of another such which followed in his reign) persisted for more than a thousand years. (Kitchen, p. 229.)

The extent of this royal family became one of the great legacies of Ramses, traceable for at least two hundred years.

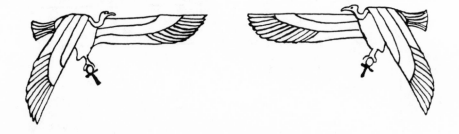

Chapter 8

The Buildings of Ramses

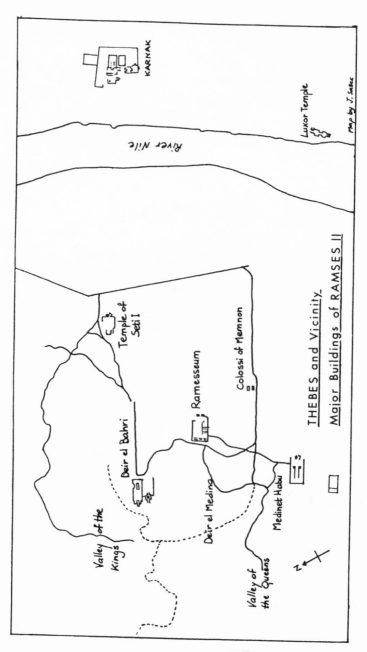

THEBES and Vicinity.
Major Buildings of RAMSES II

KARNAK

Luxor Temple

River Nile

map by J. Sales

Temple of Seti I

Ramesseum

Colossi of Memnon

Deir el Bahri

Valley of the Kings

Deir el Medina

Medinet Habu

Valley of the Queens

No. 6

The Buildings of Ramses

However skillfully Ramses might have exploited his near thing at Qadesh, or his eventual treaty with the Hittites, or his spectacular marriages, he would not have achieved the fame he did without his buildings. Seldom if ever has one ruler accounted for so remarkable a range of major buildings, some of them standing at the top of their classification. No temple anywhere can rival the Hypostyle Hall; no other royal mortuary temple stands with the Ramesseum in scale or subtlety. Of the two rock-cut temples, his Abu Simbel is surpassed in some respects only by Hatshepsut's Deir el-Bahri; in other respects, such as the impressive facade, Abu Simbel may be the more striking.

Ramses built his own buildings, and he built onto those of others, adding to temples long since under construction in Luxor, Abydos, and elsewhere. At Karnak, besides his own internal contributions he ringed the entire complex with an enormous wall.

This introduction to Ramses can only mention the major buildings by way of sketching his achievements and surmising his intentions. For on-site guidance, one would use the *Hachette World Guide,* or the excellent little guides by Jill Kamil (one called *Luxor,* or a later version called *Upper Egypt*).

The Ramesseum

Ramses located his mortuary temple west of the Nile, across the river from Luxor. He chose a spot right in a line of earlier temples, mainly from the Eighteenth Dynasty. Just before his reign began, his

father Seti had placed his own mortuary temple at Qurna, forming the northern end of this line of temples.

Ramses inserted his temple into this line, choosing a spot about one kilometer from Hatshepsut's great temple at Deir el-Bahri, and right out in front of it. He repaired some of the damage to Hatshepsut's temple done by Tuthmose III and later by Akhnaton, signing his work with a wicked grin.

The Ramesseum is a huge but very delicate building. Its proportions are superb. Its great scale was potentially dwarfed by the cliffs of Thebes to the west, and so here again the Egyptian insistence on colossal size proves itself entirely appropriate to the surroundings. A colossal statue of Ramses lies here yet. It inspired Percy Bysshe Shelley in 1818 to write his poem, "Ozymandias."

> *I met a traveller from an antique land*
> *Who said: Two vast and trunkless legs of stone*
> *Stand in the desert...Near them, on the sand,*
> *Half sunk, a shattered visage lies, whose frown*
> *And wrinkled lip, and sneer of cold command*
> *Tell that its sculptor well those passions read*
> *Which yet survive, stamped on these lifeless things...*
>
> *'My name is Ozymandias, king of kings:*
> *Look on my works, ye Mighty, and despair!'*
> *Nothing beside remains. Round the decay*
> *Of that colossal wreck, boundless and bare*
> *The lone and level sands stretch far away.*

The name Ozymandias is an ancient corruption of his throne-name, *Usi-ma-re.* Shelley's view is interesting in that he ignores the very fact of this vast complex surviving, still under the name of Ramses. But if Ramses did in fact think political power would remain within the

THE HYPOSTYLE ROOM
RAMESSEUM

framework he had set, Shelley is right that Ramses misjudged the inexorable changes wrought by time.

As with all the dynasty's buildings, the Ramesseum depicts some of the adventures of its builder. Ramses is shown at Qadesh, learning of the Hittite attack. The building is "signed" by his blocks everywhere, like most of his edifices. The characteristic royal cartouches are spread throughout the building, even on an apparent foundation stone. If only for this building, Ramses would have won lasting fame, but he also left Karnak and Abu Simbel to overshadow it.

Karnak

Back over on the eastern side of the Nile lay two more complexes to which Ramses added materially, both in building work and in the installation of his typically enormous statues.

From the Nile, the great temple of Karnak is approached through an impressive avenue of rams crouching like sphinxes. These mainly predate Ramses, but his cartouches appear on them too.

Through Pylon I, which did not exist in his day, one reaches the great court which did. To the court have since been added a large flanking temple on the south, built by Ramses III, and a small shrine of Seti II. Rows of sphinxes moved back to the sides of the court may date from Ramses II.

Straight ahead is Pylon II, done by Ramses, and through it one reaches his masterpiece, the Hypostyle Hall. Here the Egyptian combination of colossal scale and supreme refinement have combined into what was one of the "Seven Wonders of the Ancient World."

This vast hall has been variously calculated as large enough in volume to contain simultaneously St. Peter's in Rome and St. Paul's in London, or else Notre Dame in Paris.

Of its 134 columns, the twelve right before one immediately draw the eye upward to the immense height they attain, some 80 feet. Their diameter of 36 feet--about as far as six men can reach, fingertip to fingertip--causes the breath to catch. No enormous weight presses from above to require such dimensions; here the "statement" is made by the very excess to which the column builders have gone.

Since the twelve central columns soar higher than those on either side, a sort of side attic is created, as in a large cathedral. The space was filled by limestone grills to admit light and air, which poured diagonally into the vast. This "clerestory" made possible the standard basilica form so widely used ever since, including our own day.

Utilizing the light in the building, one could stroll its perimeter and gaze upon everything from a column of Ramses I to scenes of acrobats, and battle scenes both within and without. The north half of the hall celebrates Seti and his deeds, the south depicts Ramses.

A cache of thousands of statues was found about 1904 in a side court near Polon VII. It contained some of Ramses. One shows him as a ritual worshipper lying along the branch of the *ished* tree. It's a handsome thing, made of gray schist. The occasion would be celebration of the Nile flood's arrival at Thebes. (Montreal catalogue, no. 64 and back cover.)

As one wanders through a temple so vast that it can even dwarf the Hypostyle Hall, containing ten pylons and associated courts and temples as well as the sacred lake, the lesson comes home that here was a civilization which has not been superseded. This great building took

nearly two thousand years to build, if we examine the finishing touches put on by Cleopatra's father, Ptolemy Auletes. Even after Egypt passed into Roman control, the emperors embellished the building further. Even Alexander the Great and his people got in here, leaving a fine set of reliefs still on the walls of a little sanctuary beyond Pylon VI.

Luxor

If we turned right after the Hypostyle Hall rather than continuing to the eastern end of the main temple, we could emerge from the Temple of Karnak through its Tenth Pylon. That has us facing south toward Luxor, and we can follow a sphinx-lined path to the Luxor Temple.

If we looked incautiously at the facade, especially, we would conclude that Ramses alone had constructed this. In fact, a temple of some sort had stood here continuously since the Twelfth Dynasty, and it owed most of the form it had attained by the lifetime of Ramses to Amenhotep III, 75 to 100 years before. The great basilica-form construction used in the Hypostyle Hall appears already here at Luxor.

Ramses never hid his light under a bushel or anything else. As you approach the building, there rears up before you his great pylon. Before it, you encounter six great statues of himself. Two pink granite obelisks stood here; one remains, and the other has gone to Paris. The remaining one announces that Ramses has built this great temple to Amun.

Although it is Ramses that attracts people to this temple, most of the work within it predates Ramses. This was an important temple in the cult of Amun, who came here yearly during the feast of Opet, but

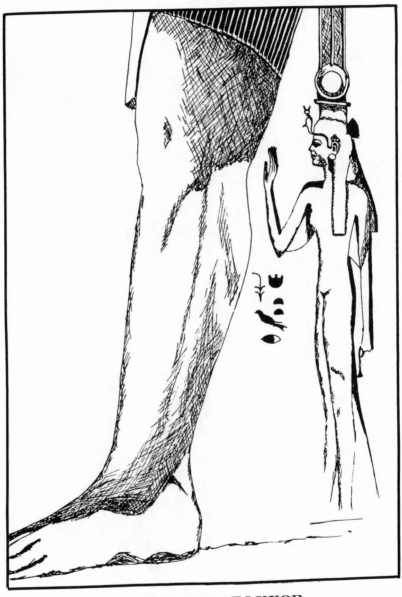

THE TEMPLE AT LUXOR
TINY CARVING OF NEFERTARI
NEAR STATUE OF RAMSES II

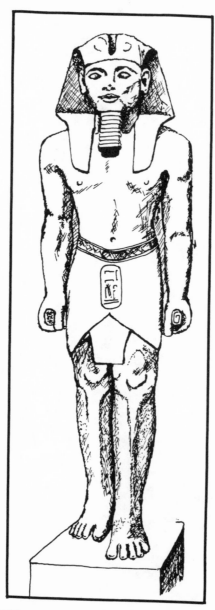

STRIDING COLOSSUS OF RAMSES II
LUXOR TEMPLE

Ramses contented himself with personal glorification out near the facade, and left his main building efforts for Karnak and Abu Simbel.

Abu Simbel

Far up the Nile, that is south on the map, and just above its waters, Ramses erected his second masterpiece. Why here? Ramses built at least six temples south of Aswan, partly of course to overawe the Nubians and remind them of Egyptian claims.

Abu Simbel lay between the first and second cataracts, some 170 miles south of Aswan, not so far from Egyptian centers of control that its possession could not be virtually guaranteed. The temple has been known to westerners since 1817, and draws more visitors than flies, especially now that they can marvel too at its rescue from the rising waters behind the Aswan High Dam.

The facade announces a theme Ramses had raised up in Luxor, where three apes appear on the remaining pink obelisk. Here at Abu Simbel, a frieze of baboons runs across the top of the facade.

All is on the usual scale. The great entrance-complex, carved from the living rock, stretches nearly 100 feet across at its base, and over 90 feet high. Four seated figures of Ramses, each some 60 feet high, stare calmly out over the Nile, as they have for 33 centuries.

The temple runs deep into the rock. Was the model Hatshepsut's temple at Deir el-Bahri? Both are cut into the rock, far back into the cliff behind, an unusual feature for an Egyptian temple. Gods, queens, family members appear throughout the great complex at Abu Simbel. Of course there are battle scenes, especially Qadesh; one scene contains over a thousand figures.

COLOSSAL STATUES OF RAMSES II
ABU SIMBEL TEMPLE

The temple stretches far into the cliff, lined with colossal figures of Ramses and the gods. Far to the rear, some hundred feet into the cliff, the sun dramatically picks out only Ramses and Amun-Re twice a year (in February and October), with light brushing Re-Harakhti on one side and Ptah on the other. The rest of the year it will illuminate other statues in various combinations.

Nefertari

There was also a special temple given to Nefertari, oriented toward the Nile like the major one. This need not date the construction of the complex to the early portion of his reign, but seems most likely to, if she was set aside later in his reign. Ramses called her "Beautiful Companion" and "his royal wife, Nefertari, whom he loves."

The Sun Sanctuary

During excavations at Abu Simbel in 1909, a representative of the Egyptian Antiquities Department discovered the most nearly complete sun-altar yet known. These had existed since early in the Old Kingdom, but only here did one survive intact. (Montreal catalogue, no. 2.) Ramses here preserved religious details two millennia old by his day, with the care he brought to any ancient continuation. The details of all this are carefully articulated to evoke not only aspects of the sun and its course, but also Re-Harakhty and Amun.

A sandstone altar supports four sacred baboons of Hermopolis, part of the four male spirits who began creation as fathers of the sun. A worshipper who had followed the clues from Luxor to Abu Simbel could now stand in the presence of this altar.

Thus far our treatment of Ramses as builder. As more traces appear in excavations especially in the Delta, we can hope for yet further information on his world. Nothing quite like this massive spurt of buildings had occurred in Egypt before; its range surpassing that of the pyramids, though they were more massive. Nothing approaching this occurred again.

Chapter 9

The Influence
of Ramses

The Libyans

One of Ramses' first services was to block the tribes west of Egypt. During the first decades of the Nineteenth Dynasty, hungry tribesmen from Libya attempted repeatedly to enter the rich northwest corner of the Delta most accessible to them. Seti resisted this on several occasions. Ramses had to face not only the familiar Meshwesh and Libu, with whom Egypt often dealt, but also more distant tribes, the Tjehenu and Tjemehu. About "year 7" he launched a raid against them, and later concluded that the danger warranted a system of fortresses.

Some of these remain visible today in the western Delta: Kom el-Barnugi, Kom el-Hisn (an Old Kingdom district capital), Kom Firin (the classical Phragonis, still unexcavated save for a brief effort in 1980-1983). In order to shield these further, Ramses erected a chain of fortress-towns along the Mediterranean coastline, stretching from the future site of Alexandria (Raqote) for some 200 miles westward.

This appears to have solved the problem for some decades, but as Ramses aged the tribes to the west pressed toward Egypt again, and in "year 5" (1232 B.C.), his successor, Merenptah, faced a very dangerous coalition of tribes. The relief his victory brought is depicted at length on the walls of Karnak.

The legacy of Ramses II had in this case required a firm reconfirmation by his son, but the Libyans' and other tribes' intention of settling in Egypt safely dissipated. How great a danger a success would have posed to Egypt can only be surmised. Since the numbers would not have sufficed for more than a partial settlement of the Delta, Egypt itself might have suffered only minimally. But an opening wedge

there could be dangerous, given the large populations roaming the coasts and seas of that period. (*CAH* II, 2, pp. 229 f.; 232 ff. Kitchen, pp. 24, 67, 71 f., 215.)

The "Exodus"

Ramses would have been astonished at the attention paid to this question. To him, the escape of a few laborers from his stock of thousands would have ranked in interest far below the day's Nilometer readings, or birth announcements from the tertiary harem.

Some of the details do ring true. Mention of a city called "Ramses" immediately suggests Pi-Ramesse in the Delta, and a number of fortress-towns using his name also existed. The so-called "Israel-stele" from the reign of Merenptah is a list of places affected adversely by the Libyan War. In part it reads:

> Destruction is for Tjehenu (mentioned above), Khatti is at peace, the Canaan is plundered...Askalon is carried off, Gezer is captured, Yenoam is made non-existent, Israel is waste and has no seed, Khor (Palestine) has become a widow because of Egypt.
>
> (*CAH* II, 2, pp. 233-234.)

For the question of a Jewish mass-escape from Egypt under Ramses, this passage may help, for it appears that a region was called Israel already in the fifth year of Merenptah. Thus the event probably occurred before he came to the throne, since five years should be too few for achieving the recognition implied by this mention.

An archaeological find helps explain the strange route that the biblical account has Moses take. Rather than proceed along the direct road from Pi-Ramesse to Gaza, and thence to his destination, he turns from the straight easterly direction he needs, and plunges south along the Gulf of Suez!

The evidence shows that a large Egyptian community stood here in the days of Ramses II. The coffins, the ornaments, the seals and scarabs and jewelry are all Egyptian; the bodies appear to be too. Gold teardrop earrings, beads, carnelian objects, alabaster goblets, items shaped for or displaying the lotus, all fit the identification. The most reliable evidence, inscriptions, has yet to emerge, but seals bear the throne-name of Ramses II, and alterations to the largest building point to his time also.

The evidence is not conclusive, but Moses may have taken the desert sojourn to avoid Egyptian garrisons like this, on the coastal road. Should it take able-bodied people forty years to cover 700 miles or so on foot? Even a spavined, weak-kneed modern city dweller can manage better than 17 miles a year or .05 miles a day. Averaged out, it would mean 500 hours to the mile.

Terrible as the Sinai desert is, could they not have used a "shallow" route and bypassed the Egyptian garrisons by only a few miles? The journey that way would be little more than 250 miles.

The Hittites

Besides his buildings and how well he got on with his wives, Ramses wins highest praise for that Hittite treaty. The "Israel stele" in fact

shows it holding even after his death. During the attack on Egypt, "Khatti is at peace." Strictly, it should have been at war on Egypt's side, but the invaders may have hit the Hittites first, and the once-great empire itself had little time left. In its weakness, it probably sought only to remain outside these theaters of war. Some evidence of agricultural troubles there further suggests weakness; as known from an inscription at Karnak, Egypt even sent grain there during a famine.

The Successors

After a great reign, the quality of the successors can be of critical importance. Ramses had so invigorated Egypt during his long reign of 67 years, and so furnished it with progeny, that no troubles with the succession proved damaging.

Ramses occupied a different tomb than originally planned, but was placed there properly by his successor. The vagaries of the future were to extract him from there again and place him in a borrowed sarcophagus in a distant chamber, but his cheerful mummy has survived all this.

Merneptah, the thirteenth son who had now reached perhaps as high as his sixties, acceded and served well, as mentioned above. Sethos II continued the tradition of Seti I and erected pillars at Karnak still visible.

Ramses III again met the "Peoples of the Sea," now more numerous and dangerous even than before. His great victory over them did not solve the problem permanently, but from then on their momentum had broken with regard to Egypt. We can see the battle in exultant detail at Medinet Habu, the building he placed at the south end of the line of temples at Thebes, balancing the Ramesseum of Ramses II in the middle and the temple of Seti I at the north end.

The increasingly obscure reigns of *Ramses IV, V, and VI* need not also be considered insignificant. The country remained stable at a time when it might easily have suffered incursions from the north and possibly the south. It was the tomb of Ramses VI which lay over the descending passage to Tutankhamun's, thus concealing it until this century.

Random finds such as a tomb-door outline and a pair of earrings assure us of the existence of descendants down to Ramses XI. By his reign, the powerful state of Ramses II was no more: Syria and Nubia were lost, internal unrest allowed even the Ramesseum's gold to be stolen, and Pi-Ramesse fell into decay.

About 1085, the priests of Amun at Thebes finally took full political power there, as Ramses had feared, and the Twenty-First Dynasty signalled the end of the New Kingdom. Priests, and princes from Tanis, divided the country's rule.

Let it be remembered, however, that Egypt retained its identity far longer. After a century under the new dynasty, it came under the rule of Libyans, another old fear revived, and 150 years after that it fell to Nubians, the last of the traditional enemies. Behind then came a dreary file of foreign conquerors--Assyrians, Persians, Greeks, Romans, Byzantines. Only briefly did it re-emerge into self-government, in the Twenty-Sixth Dynasty and again in the Thirtieth.

Egyptians never lost their spirit: one great old story has a king from this last dynasty surreptitiously manage to father Alexander the Great on a trip up north. This has the desirable effect of making "legitimate"

the next dynasty to rule Egypt. Cleopatra, the last of that line, must have heard the story. At any rate, there's no doubt that she sincerely believed herself of Egyptian lineage, and ultimately thought herself a reincarnation of the Goddess Isis.

Conclusion

The success of the Ramses Exhibition in Paris in 1976, then beginning a new cycle of three cities at Montreal in 1985, points up an interesting difference with the Tutankhamun Exhibit in London, Seattle, and elsewhere. The Tut Exhibit comes out of an unrifled tomb; marvellous objects, completely fresh, are there in practically the same condition as when new. A wide range of items from the gold sarcophagus down to minor pins makes his treasure nearly inexhaustible.

By contrast, Ramses has left us little. No golden sarcophagus, no gold face mask, no daggers of precious metal. The violation of tomb probably just before 1000 B.C. removed all of the spectacular items the thieves could conveniently take up. By comparison with Tut, a boy who had reigned less than ten years and accomplished little, what must Ramses have possessed, after 67 years of war and building?

Yet a few fine items have come down, like the golden bracelets

bearing Ramses' name found in 1906 at Bubastis (Montreal catalogue, no. 23.), or some of his jewelry in the Louvre. Other superb items found in the temples, especially at Karnak and in the Ramesseum, increase the collection to more than respectable dimension.

The crowds don't care anyway. They come in vast numbers to either of these collections. Why do they come? Even those who profess no prior knowledge of Ramses in particular show up with eager expressions. What do they expect?

Antiquity. This on a scale seldom available outside Egypt or Mesopotamia. Here you have a man with known wives, children, deeds, words--and he walked around his court in 1250 B.C. At that time, North and South America, and most of Europe were in the hunter-gatherer mode, by comparison. Some respectable rudiments, yes, but you had to get down toward the Mediterranean for a solid civilization and the luxuries people associate with it. What they were groping toward, Egypt had already had--for centuries.

Achievement. Any tourist in Egypt will see evidence of Ramses at virtually every turn. In the Delta, it has been obscured by the destruction and buildup of soil, but it's there, in every ancient town and in most of the farmers' fields. The little *ushabti* figurines, of Ramses in particular, turn up very frequently. As you move southward, his very buildings and obelisks and sphinxes appear, by the time you reach Abydos, Thebes, Karnak, Luxor, Abu Simbel.

There must be no other figure in history who has left such a plethora of great buildings. Certainly not Ur-Nammu, Hammurabi, Pericles, Alexander, Caesar, Augustus, Hadrian, Charlemagne, Napoleon. The only serious rival would be the Byzantine Emperor Justinian. His geographical range exceeded that of Ramses, from Haghia Sophia in Istanbul to several in Italy, with others in Asia Minor and North Africa. But these are "merely" exquisite buildings. Haghia Sophia is enormous, too, but not on the Egyptian scale.

In buildings resides the greatest claim of Ramses, but it should be added that he saw dangers and held them back while this program of building progressed. In centuries ahead, he was to be proved correct in every case but one of the apprehensions he held. The Libyans were a danger, and one day they ruled Egypt (Dyn. XX-XXIV). The Nubians should be watched; sure enough they ruled Egypt as well (Dyn. XXV). The priests of Amun could be tricky, he said, and here they came as the local successors of the Ramessids, 150 years after his death.

Only with the Hittites did he prove unnecessarily wary. As matters developed, they stuck to their treaty throughout his lifetime and beyond. Their empire collapsed, in the twelfth century, and they threatened Egypt no more.

Tradition. Ramses saw the value of Egypt's long past more clearly than almost any other pharaoh, saving perhaps his father, Seti. Both realized that the awesome successions of priests and kings recorded throughout the land worked in their favor. Enlist the people in a great effort to remain true to that long commitment, fill the bellies of the workmen, give them all a share in the great construction efforts, and they will smile upon you, as we know they did.

The new dynasty of the Ramessids was the best thing that could happen to Egypt, as the great Eighteenth Dynasty crumbled. Seldom have three individuals--Ramses I, Seti I, Ramses II--risen so strongly to the occasion. Egypt smiled for most of 250 years largely because of them, and the modern visitor can smile still.

Bibliography

A full bibliography of the subject of this book would be enormous. The best place to start for specific questions is the chapter-by-chapter bibliographies in the third edition (1970 onward) of *The Cambridge Ancient History* [Hereafter: CAH], especially Vol. II, 1-2, and in the notes to the best specific treatment of Ramses II, K.A. Kitchen, *Pharaoh Triumphant: The Life and Times of Ramesses II, King of Egypt* (Aris & Phillips, Ltd., Warminster, England, 1982). [Hereafter: Kitchen.] J.D. Schmidt also provides a good bibliography.

The following are useful for the present book and as an introduction to its subject matter.

Baines, J., and Malek, J., *Atlas of Ancient Egypt* (Oxford and New York 1980; Equinox.) [Hereafter: Baines and Malek.]

Breasted, J.H., *Ancient Records of Egypt*, I-V (Chicago 1905-1907). [Usually abbreviated BAR.]

Breasted, J.H., *A History of the Ancient Egyptians* (New York 1905 and 1908).

Gardiner, Sir Alan, *Egypt of the Pharaohs* (Oxford 1961). Still an authoritative treatment. [Hereafter: Gardiner.]

James, T.G.H., *An Introduction to Ancient Egypt* (British Museum, 1979; London and New York).

Kitchen, K.A., *Ramesside Inscriptions*, I-VII (Oxford 1968 ff.).

Kitchen, K.A., *The Egyptian Nineteenth Dynasty*, (1984).

Montet, P., *Eternal Egypt*, (1964; Mentor paperback 1968), the most readable short introduction to Egypt, by a respected excavator.

Porter, B., and Moss, R.L.B., *Topographical Bibliography of Ancient Egyptian Hieroglyphic Texts, Reliefs, and Paintings*, I-VII (Oxford 1927-1951; second edition began in 1960). The fundamental study of the ancient sites, identified by their names in the texts and inscriptions.

Romer, John, *Ancient Lives: Daily Life in Egypt of the Pharaohs* (New York 1984), dealing with Deir el Medina. [Hereafter: Romer.]

Schmidt, J.D., *Ramesses II: A Chronological Structure for His Reign* (Baltimore 1973). Attention to the literary, astronomical (lunar and Sothic), and epigraphical evidence.

Seele, K.C., *The Coregency of Ramses II with Seti I and the Date of the Great Hypostyle Hall at Karnak* (Chicago 1940).

Settipani, M., in *Heraldique et genealogie*, c. 1984 [non vidi], traces dynastic claims of descent from Ramses on into the Middle Ages--an indication of his strong reputation, at least.

Steindorff, G., and Seele, K., *When Egypt Ruled the East* (Chicago 1942; ed. 2, 1957). [Hereafter: Steindorff and Seele.]

Wilson, J.A., *The Burden of Egypt* (Chicago 1951; paperback edition 1956 under the title, *The Culture of Ancient Egypt*).